MW01127213

The Christian Lifestyle:

Paul's Letter to the Philippians

By

Dale L. Rowley

ISBN-13: 978-1456522513

Contents

Copyright Acknowledgments
Foreword
Dedication

Copyright Acknowledgments

Forward

This book is a study in the New Testament book, Philippians. It is designed to be a guide for individual study or small group discussions, helping Christians gain a more fulfilling spiritual life through understanding the nature of Christian transformation. This book is not designed as a study for the Bible scholar; it is designed for the average Christian seeking to understand more about the Christian life and how to live more abundantly. The author does not claim to be a New Testament scholar, however he is able to research the Scriptures sufficiently to get at the deeper meanings. The author hopes the study of this book will save the readers many hours of research on their own.

The author takes full credit, and/or, blame for the editing of the final manuscript. There are some inconsistencies on how various verses are referred to, depending on the nature of how they are used in paragraphs. The author is greatly indebted to many different sites on the Internet as well as the BibleSoft® program, *PC Bible,* a computer program for Bible study. The author gratefully acknowledges his dependence on several different translations of the New Testament.

The study questions at the end of the book, divided by chapters, were written by the author and designed to help the reader think more deeply and personally about the lessons found in the Bible passages. They are appropriate for small group discussions as well as individual devotional thoughts.

Different authors choose to, or not to, capitalize pronouns referring to deity. This is true of general religious works as well as different translations of the Bible. This author has chosen to capitalize those pronouns to help clarify their antecedents. Bible quotes reflect the usage in the translation used.

The author has chosen to use bold type for scripture passage and words, as long as they are not too repetitious, to help the reader follow the segment being discussed.

To my precious wife,
Dena,
without whom my life
would be terribly short on
meaning and joy.

CHAPTER 1

ꓕ Lifestyle of Sainthood

Phil 1:1-2 NIV **Paul and Timothy, servants of Christ Jesus, To all the saints in Christ Jesus at Philippi, together with the overseers and deacons: 2 Grace and peace to you from God our Father and the Lord Jesus Christ.**

Paul addresses his readers **to all the saints in Christ Jesus who are in Philippi**. The word translated **saints** is in the Greek, *hagios* (hag'-ee-os). This is the New Testament equivalent of a Hebrew word meaning "to separate" or "to set apart." Thus, Paul is acknowledging the special position held by believers in Jesus Christ. The word refers to those things that are holy and sacred. We are different from the world, having been transformed by the power of Christ. Paul is writing to all the Christians in the church.

Paul visited **Philippi** on his second missionary journey in approximately 52 AD. There was no church or synagogue when he arrived, so he met with some women worshiping down by a river. After explaining the gospel, he baptized Lydia and some of the other women. Later, Paul cast out a demon from a young girl with the spirit of divination (fortune-telling). Paul and Silas were scourged and thrown into prison; an earthquake set them free, the magistrates repented their treatment of men who were Roman citizens and begged them to leave the city. A prison guard and his family became Christians because of this event. When Paul left, no other Christians were mentioned. However, it is obvious that others were added to the church in Paul's absence. The whole story is found in Acts 16:12-40.

Paul specifically addressed **overseers and deacons**. Let us look at these two words. The word here translated **overseers** is *episkopos* (ep-is'-kop-os). You will quickly notice the kinship

1

to the word "Episcopalian." The word is often translated "Bishop." It is from this concept that the Episcopal style of church government is taken. This is where there is a hierarchy of church authority. In the Roman Catholic Church this authority begins with the Pope and filters downward. Several denominations follow this pattern, although only the Roman Catholic Church has a Pope.

Many other denominations view the **overseer** as a guide and mentor, rather than an authority figure. They have a more democratic form of church government.

The word here translated **deacons**, is *diakonos* (dee-ak'-on-os). It is most often translated a "minister" or "servant." And here, in the word itself, we see the primary qualification for the office of deacon. You may find other qualifications in 1 Tim. 3:8ff.

Deacons, as Christian lay people, share the shepherding task of the pastor. A pastor is different from a preacher. The word "pastor" pictures a shepherd taking care of his sheep. Some sheep are lost. Others are injured. Still, others are sick or dying. Others are being born. We live in a world of pain. Our world is full of people who are "laughing on the outside but crying on the inside." *Trouble* is the common denominator of humanity. Some pains are physical and quite observable. Others are emotional and kept well hidden.

Here is a message to deacons. As a lay person, you serve (minister) in the name of Christ. You have every emotion other people have. As you have learned to handle your struggles through the grace of Christ, you can help other people to do likewise. As you accept your humanity, you can help your friends to accept theirs. There are all kinds of mishaps in their lives. Sometimes, in ill health, their body becomes their enemy. In some families, a spouse, a child, or an aging parent becomes a source of unbearable burdens. At times it's one's job, or friends, or fears, or loneliness, or sense of failure. Why? Because we are all human. Accepting your own humanity and that of other people will enable you to reach out in ministry.

Notice the tender, upbeat note on which Paul begins this letter. **Grace and peace to you from God our Father and the Lord Jesus Christ. Grace** is a word that is broad in scope. It includes many things: the notion of acceptance, the concept of

2

being favored by God, the thought of being set free, and the property of being filled with thanksgiving. Many of us, learned the definition of **grace** as "unmerited favor." That is, receiving a gift that we did not deserve. That refers to the gift of Christ that provides us with forgiveness and everlasting life. **Grace** is the translation of the Greek word *charis* (khar'-ece). **Grace** has at least three dimensions. It is the gift of God that provides for salvation. The second dimension is that divine strength that allows us to suffer for Christ's sake and continue to propagate the gospel. The third dimension is the quality of life displayed by the person who has been transformed by Christ, that is, living a life filled with grace. As Christians, we extend **grace** to others.

Peace is more than inner composure. It includes the meaning of a restored fellowship between man and God on the basis of Christ's forgiveness. This inward **peace** springs from knowing you have been saved by God's **grace**. Clearly, **grace and peace** come from **God our Father and the Lord Jesus Christ**. The apostle succinctly states two relationships: first, **God** is our **Father**, and second, **Jesus Christ** is our **Lord**.

The **God** of which Paul speaks is the **God** of the Hebrew nation. We usually perceive **God** as the supernatural creator and overseer of the universe. Through the years, theologians have spoken of God as omniscient (having all knowledge), omnipotent (having complete power), omnipresent (being present everywhere), omnibenevolent (having perfect goodness). This is the **God** of three major religions: Christianity, Judaism, and Islam.

The concept of God as **Father** is ancient and shared by many religions. God as the creator, is the father of all. To Christians, God the Father's relationship with humanity is as a Father to His spiritual children (see Matt. 6:9). So Christians are often referred to as "children of God."

It is only natural for us to try to conceive of God in human terms. This is called anthropomorphism. The term is derived from a combination of the Greek *anthropos* (anth'-ro-pos), "human" and *morphe* (mor-fay'), "shape" or "form." However, we must be reminded that ultimately God and His ways are beyond all human understanding (see Isaiah 55:8-9).

The **Lord Jesus Christ** is hereby given as the second source of **grace and peace**. This is a reminder of the salvation brought by **Jesus Christ** and His death, burial, and resurrection. Without this event, there would be no eternal life for mankind. He was God's perfect sacrifice for our sins.

Paul does not here mention the third person of the Godhead. That is the Holy Spirit. In Christianity, we recognize God the Father, God the Son, and God the Holy Spirit. This relationship has often been called the "Trinity." It is probably better described by the word "Triunity." This better portrays the idea of three in one. Explaining this difficult doctrine defies human understanding. We accept it by faith.

We are here reminded that each of us is to live like a saint, one who is set apart from the world, living for Christ.

I offer this paraphrase of Phil 1:1-2. **Paul and Timothy, who are servants of Christ, are together writing this letter. I, Paul, am addressing it to all my consecrated brothers and sisters at Philippi. Of course, I include all the deacons and elders in this group. We pray that God's blessing and peace will be with you in every way** (DLR).

CHAPTER 2

ꟼ Lifestyle of Continuity

While Paul was in a Roman prison, a dear friend from years gone by, came to visit him. The friend was Epaphroditus. He brought a gift from the church at Philippi. His arrival reminded Paul of all of his dear friends in that church. He decided to send a letter back with Epaphroditus. Philippians is that letter.

Phil 1:3-8 CEV **Every time I think of you, I thank my God. 4 And whenever I mention you in my prayers, it makes me happy. 5 This is because you have taken part with me in spreading the good news from the first day you heard about it. 6 God is the one who began this good work in you, and I am certain that he won't stop before it is complete on the day that Christ Jesus returns. 7 You have a special place in my heart. So it is only natural for me to feel the way I do. All of you have helped in the work that God has given me, as I defend the good news and tell about it here in jail. 8 God himself knows how much I want to see you. He knows that I care for you in the same way that Christ Jesus does.**

Verse 3. **Every time I think of you, I thank my God**. Eugene Peterson embellishes this phrase in this way, **Every time you cross my mind, I break out in exclamations of thanks to God** (MSG). The Greek word for **thanks** is *eucharisteo* (yoo-khar-is-teh'-o). You may recognize this as the basis for the English word "Eucharist." In several Christian denominations, this word is used for Communion or the Lord's Supper. This implies gratitude for the sacrifice that provides our salvation. The word for **remembrance** (KJV) is *mneia* (mni'-ah). Those of you who studied psychology should remember the concept and practice of using mnemonic (the *m* is silent) devices as memory aids. You musicians, very early in your musical career, most likely learned this mnemonic device. "**E**very **G**ood **B**oy **D**oes **F**ine" to learn those treble clef notes on the lines, and "**FACE**" to learn those spaces. For Paul the word "Philippi" reminded him of his dear friends at Philippi. As we look at verse five, **have taken part with** me, is a translation of the Greek word *koinonia* (koy-nohn-ee'-ah). It comes from a verb meaning "to have in common." Many translations translate this "fellowship." We are all part of the family of God. The phrase **from the first day** is obviously a reference to the beginning of Paul's ministry to the church at Philippi (cf. Acts 16:12 ff). Verse 6. **Being confident of this very thing** (KJV). **Confident** comes from a verb meaning to convince. Here Paul is convinced of the truth of that which is to follow, namely, **certain that he won't stop before it is complete**. God will continue working His good in the believer. Everyone has a history. Everyone has regrets. Everyone's past accuses him of misdeeds. Failure has produced its share of guilt. However, the story doesn't end there. The potential for growth goes on. One can always make the best of a bad situation. God's forgiveness stands in the wings. This process begins with putting the past behind you. Yes. You made some mistakes. Yes. You ignored God's teachings in your life. You ignored the advice of others. When you get quiet at night, your thoughts go back to those unhappy times. Tears may flow. Yet, the past is past. It is time to accept God's forgiveness and forgive yourself. Then move ahead. That brings us to the present day-to-day living. Living one day at a time is the goal here. No regrets from the past. No borrowed troubles from the future. Making the most of today's struggles. Capturing this day's pleasures. Counting your blessings. In a renewed fashion, dedicate yourself to God. Accept His forgiveness. Sit back and let God work in your life. He'll surprise you. He really will! This is God making **complete** the **good work** He began in us.

Do you ever get the feeling that you will never become all that God wants you to be? Have you a weakness you just can't quite overcome? Have you a habit you cannot break? Have you a task you keep putting off? Have you a calling that you have resisted and not fulfilled? Paul is assuring his Philippian friends that, when we trust God, He will make the believer victorious in the end. Paul is saying that the **good work began** through their faith in Christ is designed to be carried on to completion. That ultimate completion is brought about on **the day that Christ Jesus returns**. This refers to the second coming as in Phil. 1:10. Paul never sets the time for the Lord's return, but he is inspired by that marvelous expectation. In verse seven, Paul says, **you have a special place in my heart**. The word for "heart" here is *kardia* (kar-dee'-ah). You will note the English words that come from this: cardiac, cardiologist. The Greek word refers to the heart, liver, and lungs, thus the center of life. In the Bible, it refers to both physical and spiritual life. **So it is only natural for me to feel the way I do**. As we look at the passage up to this point, we find Paul speaking of his thanksgiving, his joy, and his confidence. Paul further justifies his love for the Philippian people by observing, **All of you have helped in the work that God has given me.** This is sometimes translated as "partakers" and carries the implication of "joint partner." The NIV translates this **all of you share in God's grace with me**. **Grace** translates the Greek word *charis* (khar'-ece). We looked at this word in verse 1:2.

Here in jail clearly establishes that this letter was written from prison. Paul was in what we would call "house arrest." In a room somewhere, there were always guards present. If he went outside for exercise, he was accompanied by guards. He was permitted to have visitors and have certain needs provided by them.

As I defend the good news declares Paul's faithfulness in sharing the message. The word for "good news" is *euaggelion*, (yoo-ang-ghel'-ee-on). You can see the cognate "evangelism." The word itself has a simple translation: "the good news." This refers to the good news that Jesus saves.

In verse eight, Paul says his love comes from the heart of Christ Jesus himself. **I care for you** translates a Greek prepositional phrase, literally "with the entrails of Christ." The entrails, in this Greek word, consist of the spleen and bowels. In biblical times these were collectively regarded as the seat of feelings and affections, the equivalent of "heart" in modern usage. Paul identifies himself so closely with Christ that the deep feeling he has toward his Christian friends appears to be nothing other than the love of Christ himself.

Christians, for years have been both puzzled by and embarrassed by the King James translation, **I long after you all in the bowels of Jesus Christ** (KJV). Perhaps that was less offensive in 1611. It is an accurate translation, however, it uses terminology that is not used in the 20th or 21st centuries. Paul is saying that he cares for the Philippians the **same way** that Christ cares for them.

This is a good place to make some comments about translation. Translators do not just translate words, but they translate ideas. In this passage just discussed, the KJV translates the words accurately. However, because of cultural changes, all modern translations translate the idea rather than the specific words.

What a blessing it is, to be a part of the family of God. Within this family are some of the finest people on earth. To love them and be loved by them is richly rewarding. We are part of a family that never ends.

Here is my paraphrase of 1:3-8. **I thank God for your memory every time you cross my mind. I find great joy in every occasion that I can pray for you. I can't help but remember how, from the very beginning, you have helped me spread the good news. God began a good work in you. I am convinced He will continue working in you until He is satisfied with the finished product. That will be on the day Christ returns. You have a special place in my heart. It is like we are one with each other because of God's grace. I even feel your strength upholding me as I share the good news here in jail. I sure would like to see all of you. I love you dearly as Christ loves you through me** (DLR).

CHAPTER 3

A Lifestyle of Right Living

A small boy was being especially hateful to his younger sister. His exasperated mother said to him, "Johnny, the devil made you push and kick your sister!"

Johnny replied, "Well, the devil may have made me push and kick her, but pulling her hair was my own idea." This portion of Paul's letter is about knowing right from wrong and choosing to do right.

Phil 1:9-11 NASU **And this I pray, that your love may abound still more and more in real knowledge and all discernment, 10 so that you may approve the things that are excellent, in order to be sincere and blameless until the day of Christ; 11 having been filled with the fruit of righteousness which comes through Jesus Christ, to the glory and praise of God.**

Paul often let his friends know that he prayed for them. In this way, he taught them the importance of prayer and how to pray. In this prayer, Paul expected his readers to experience growth in the faith. Herein is a lesson for the 21st century. We ought to pray for each other. We note here that these Philippians, who were already experienced in love, knowledge, and discernment still had room for growth in all areas. The lesson here is that we are all imperfect and need further growth in our Christian experience. There is room for improvement in our best accomplishments.

The word **love** used in verse 9 is the noun *agape* (ag-ah'-pay). It refers to the high degree of spiritual warmth that God has for His human children and the deep affection that they, in turn, should have for Him and each other. Because of the hundreds of references to **love** in the Bible, it is impossible in this writing, to consider all of its uses. At a minimum, it means these things: we are to love God, and one another, and all people. Living a life of love fulfills both the Old Testament law and the New Testament gospel.

We are reminded of the conversation between Jesus and the lawyer of His day. Matt 22:36-40 NKJV **"Teacher, which is the great commandment in the law?" 37 Jesus said to him, "'You shall love the LORD your God with all your heart, with all your soul, and with all your mind.' 38 This is the first and great commandment. 39 And the second is like it: 'You shall love your neighbor as yourself.' 40 On these two commandments hang all the Law and the Prophets."**

Of special interest is the difference between the two words used for **love** in the New Testament. (A third Greek word, *eros*, describing erotic love is not used in the Bible.) We looked at *agape*, the other word is *phileo* (fil-eh'-o). It is a less intense and dedicated kind of love. The difference between the two is most clearly illustrated in our Lord's interview with Simon Peter following His resurrection (John 21:15-19). When Jesus says, "Do you love me?" He uses the Greek word *agape*.

When Simon answers, "Yes, I love you," he uses the Greek word *phileo*. These words are used this way in the first and second questions asked by Jesus. When Jesus asked the question the third time, he also used the word *phileo*.

In this interchange, we see Jesus asking Peter for a deeper, stronger kind of love than Peter is able to give. So, Jesus comes down to his level. A more accurate translation of the first two questions in this dialogue would be, "Simon, do you really love me deeply?"

And Peter's response, "Lord, you know, I am your dear friend."

The third question would be, "Simon, are you really my close friend?"

Peter responds, "Lord, you know all things. You know that I am your close friend." This distinction is found in the TLB, AMP, and some other versions.

Knowledge and all discernment. True **knowledge** and careful **discernment** (some translations use **judgment** KJV, TEV) are essential elements of love. **Love** should keep on growing (implied in the Greek present tense). Love should

10

develop into, and be accompanied by, spiritual and moral insights. Each person is to grow in God's love and grace until his influence reaches outside himself and touches the lives of others. The word translated **discernment** is frequently used by Paul to suggest a comprehensive grasp of spiritual truth. Christ's followers should diligently seek the truth in all matters.

Verse 10 is a continuation of the kind of love Paul prays his readers will have. He wants them to **approve the things that are excellent**. He wants them to choose what is best in all situations.

Sincere and blameless translates the word *eilikrines* (i-lik-ree-nace') meaning "judged by sunlight." Picture a merchant receiving a gold coin in a dark room. To better evaluate its genuineness, the merchant takes it out into the sunlight to get a better view.

Let us note the English word "sincere," which comes from the Latin *sin* "without" and *ceres* "spoilage." *Without spoilage.* Picture with me a first century Roman lady grocery shopping at the local street market. She comes up to a vendor who sells squash, melons, apples and a variety of other fruits and vegetables. A sign on top of select piles of merchandise reads, "Sin Ceres." No rotten spots. No hidden blemishes. No fancy cover-ups. If it looks good, it is good. Jesus wants us to be **sincere**. No phoniness. No pretense. No deception. No hypocrisy. "What you see is what you get."

Until the day of Christ. Paul seems to have in mind the fitness of the Philippians to stand before Christ on the Day of Judgment. Our sincerity and good judgment, brought about by our faith in Christ, is to prepare us for this event.

Verse 11 continues the qualifications Paul looks for in a mature Christian. **Having been filled with the fruit of righteousness which comes through Jesus Christ**. This word for **righteousness** includes having a right standing with God through faith in Jesus Christ and doing the right things. It is a word that refers to Christian character or actions.

This phrase reminds us that the source of righteousness in the Christian life is our belief in Jesus Christ. There is no righteousness outside of Him. **This righteousness from God comes through faith in Jesus Christ to all who believe** (Rom 3:22 NIV). And when we have the righteousness that He

11

provides, we bear certain kinds of fruit. By **righteousness** we include the total transformation by the Spirit of God, and the altered life that transformation produces.

In Galatians 5:22-23, Paul writes of the fruit of the Spirit as the expectation for those living the Christian life. **22 But the fruit of the Spirit is love, joy, peace, patience, kindness, goodness, faithfulness, 23 gentleness, self-control; against such things there is no law** (NASU).

In our Christian life, we are to be noticed for righteous living. We are not to be like those in this joke. A rancher asked a veterinarian for some free advice. "I have a horse," he said, "that walks normally sometimes and limps sometimes. What shall I do?"

The veterinarian replied, "The next time he walks normally, sell him."

The end goal of the Christian life is for every child of God to bring about the **glory and praise of God**. The word **glory** refers to the kingly majesty that belongs to God as supreme ruler. This **glory** suggests the absolute splendor of the eternal God. **Glory** translates the Greek word, *doxa* (dox'-ah). Do you see where *The Doxology* gets its name?

Here is my paraphrase of Phil 1:9-11. **I pray that your love and understanding will keep on growing. I pray you will know the difference between right and wrong and always choose the right. If you do that, you will be pure and innocent when Christ returns. Until that day arrives, Christ will use you daily in His service. Our goal is to bring glory and praise to God. He deserves it** (DLR).

ʎ Lifestyle of Perseverance

**Phil 1:12-14 TEV I want you to know, my friends, that the
things that have happened to me have really helped the
progress of the gospel. 13 As a result, the whole palace
guard and all the others here know that I am in prison
because I am a servant of Christ. 14 And my being in
prison has given most of the believers more confidence in
the Lord, so that they grow bolder all the time to preach
the message fearlessly.**

Let us look at the word **friends**; it is **brothers** in the NIV and
others. There is hardly a higher compliment for a Christian
than to be called a Christian friend or brother. As in this case,
Paul most often used the word **brother** in the sense of a fellow
Christian. For a Christian to call another Christian "brother" is
to express affection. This word comes from the Greek word
adelphos (ad-el-fos'). In verse nine, we looked at the Greek
word *phileo* (fil-eh'-o). Put this together with *adelphos*, and we
have the source of "Philadelphia," the city of "brotherly love."
We looked at this Greek word *adelphos* (ad-el-fos') in verse
1:12. Here we will look at it a little deeper. Several translations
use a generic term **friends**. This is seen in the TLB, MSG, and
the CEV. Others translate it gender inclusive as **my brothers
and sisters** (NCV, NLT). The root form of *adelphos* is *a*
meaning "from"and *delphos* meaning "the womb." Well, it does
not take too much ingenuity to recognize that both males and
females come from the womb. But, because both the New
Testament and Old Testament cultures were male dominated,
it is usually translated **brothers**. It is frequently used in the
feminine to specifically designate a "sister." It is most often
masculine in the Greek. When this word does not specifically
address a male, it could properly reflect the idea of "siblings."
When referring to people, the masculine gender is the gender
customarily used in Greek. When used in the plural, the

masculine will be used for groups composed of both genders. Many believe the status of women in 21st century America justifies their inclusion in this word. We assume this letter was written to the women in the church as well as the men.

The word for **helped the progress of the gospel** uses the concept of "profitability." It is sometimes used in the business sense. Paul sees this jailhouse experience as something that will further the gospel. In that way, his being in jail is a profitable experience.

I met many prisoners who believed going to jail was the best thing that happened to them, for different reasons than the apostle Paul. Many found it an opportunity and challenge to rethink their lives and the direction they were taking. I frequently heard, "If I were not in jail, I would be dead." Several prisoners also found this an opportunity to accept Christ as their Savior and begin living in a new direction.

Let us note here that it is common to find the gospel being spread more readily under persecution than in open freedom. In this 21st century, China is a good example of this.

A Christian missionary tells of witnessing a Chinese father, baptizing his 15-year-old daughter. He asked her four questions: (1) Do you believe in Jesus? (2) Has He forgiven your sins? (3) Do you promise to walk with Him always? And then the fourth, very penetrating question, (4) When they come into our house and take us away, when they beat us and try to get us to deny Him, will you still follow Jesus?

Here, let us note, the nature of Paul's imprisonment. He was not in a dungeon, as he had been in Philippi. Rather, he was placed in the modern day equivalent of "house arrest." That is, he was confined to a given house, and, if he went outside for exercise or any other reason, he was continuously chained to, or accompanied by, a Roman guard. This arrangement allowed him to receive visitors, which he apparently did on several occasions. We would also note that his being constantly observed by a Roman guard gave him a captive audience for sharing the message of Christ. As a succession of soldiers came to guard him, they heard the message of Christ. Apparently many became believers. In Phil 4:22, Paul writes, **All the saints salute you, chiefly they that are of Caesar's household** (KJV). From this, we see that the influence of Christianity had reached some of the higher-ups in the emperor's palace. Perhaps, even some of the family of the emperor had been converted.

The whole palace guard and all the others here know that I am in prison because I am a servant of Christ. It apparently did not take long for the guards to realize that Paul was not a typical criminal. Rather, he was in prison because he preached Christ. If he had not been a Christian, and had not appealed to Caesar on this religious matter, he would not be in prison. The matter of his innocence became common knowledge among the Roman guards and filtered up to the family of Caesar himself.

Whole palace guard translates the Greek word *praitorion* (prahee-to'-ree-on). It is often translated **palace**. Paul is probably relating to the **palace** in which the governor or procurator of Rome resided. It sometimes referred to the tent of the commander-in-chief of the local army.

The word **Lord** translates the Greek *kurios* (koo'-ree-os). It may refer to the owner of land or owner of slaves. It is a title of respect with which servants would greet their master. And, as here, it is a title given to divinity.

A more literal translation for **preach the message** is **speak the word** (KJV). The Greek word translating **word** is *logos* (log'-os). It is a word with many translations. Literally it means "a spoken or written word," and is most often translated that way. It can also mean a **message**. We look particularly at John 1:1-3. **In the beginning was the Word, and the Word was with God, and the Word was God. 2 He was in the beginning with God. 3 All things were made through Him, and without Him nothing was made that was made** (NKJV). In this passage, the word *logos* clearly refers to Jesus Christ the Son of God. He is the eternal **message** of God.

The word for **confidence** implies these converts were convinced by argument that Jesus Christ was the Son of God. These were not flippant decisions. They were the result of deliberation and study.

Fearlessly is the negative of the Greek word *phobos* (fob'-oce). You can quickly see several cognates from this word. Here are a few that relate to church and religion; fear of religious ceremonies, – teleophobia; church – ecclesiophobia; crucifix, the or crosses – staurophobia; death or dying – thanatophobia; religion or gods – theophobia; and then – the

15

number – 666, hexakosioihexekontahexaphobia. (Aren't words fun?)

Here we see the apostle Paul saying that his imprisonment has made many followers of Christ **grow bolder**. A common, searching question comes early in life as children meet pain and at least occasional deprivation. "Why must I face hardships in my life?" For the Christian, the question includes the element of faith. "Why does God not deliver me from this pain, sorrow, or difficulty?" "Why me, Lord?" "Why do good people have to suffer?" The question is as old as the righteous Job who said, **I have no peace or quiet. I cannot rest, I am in such turmoil** (Job 3:26 DLR).

In times of crises, we need *eyes of faith.* A person in distress can see more clearly with such eyes. Eyes of faith allow us to see God and good, even when others can see only tragedy and hopelessness. With eyes of faith, people look up when things go wrong. They know God has not forsaken them. They know they are not alone. People of faith use their tragedy as a springboard to a closer walk with Christ.

Philippians 1:12-14 can be paraphrased this way. **I want you to know, my brothers and sisters, that my being in jail has really turned out for the good. It has helped to spread the gospel. The guards and everyone else knows I am in prison only because I believe in Christ. And because I am in prison, other Christians are more bold in their witness** (DLR).

CHAPTER 5

A Lifestyle of Pure Motives

Most people have been in a contest of some sort, perhaps a school election or a foot race; or perhaps a contest to see who could bring the best food to a potluck or a chili cook-off. On those occasions, did we not relish the bad luck of our opponent? Were we not happy to see them fail in some measure, that we might win? That seems to be human nature.

Now, imagine with me, some Christian preachers in Rome were trying to build a congregation, then Paul appears on the scene, a recognized authority regarding the gospel. His reputation attracts people to hear him. Now, some of those jealous preachers, probably spoke among themselves saying, "Well I'm glad he's in jail. That doesn't look too good. At least he'll be limited in his influence." That would give them better opportunity to steal people's affections and establish themselves as the bona fide preachers of the gospel. Not a lot is known about these preachers, but it is clear that they are "pro-Christ" but "anti-Paul." Let's read about them.

Phil 1:15-17 NIV **It is true that some preach Christ out of envy and rivalry, but others out of goodwill. 16 The latter do so in love, knowing that I am put here for the defense of the gospel. 17 The former preach Christ out of selfish ambition, not sincerely, supposing that they can stir up trouble for me while I am in chains.**

Remember the saying, "We blow out the other fellow's candle when a shines more brightly than our own." This appears to be the motives of some of the preachers who disliked Paul.

In the 2009 playoff between the Los Angeles Dodgers and the St. Louis Cardinals, the Cardinals led two to one in the ninth inning. There were two outs. A fly ball came to a Cardinal outfielder. Catching the ball would mean a victory for the

Cardinals. But, he dropped the ball, ultimately causing a Cardinal loss. After the game, the player said, "I couldn't see the ball, I lost it in the lights. You come in for the ball, get a good read on it, but at the last minute I lost it in the lights. It hit my body, hit my glove, unfortunate timing. It wasn't because of lack of effort. I just couldn't see the ball." He surely felt terrible. But can't you see the LA Dodgers jumping up and down and cheering. They were happy at the failure and misfortune of another.

Paul does not clarify what he meant by **out of envy and rivalry.** It appears that in Rome there was a party that was jealous of the influence of Paul. Several commentaries suggest that they were likely Judaizers, Jewish Christians who wanted to retain many of the Jewish practices, particularly insisting Gentiles should be circumcised before becoming Christians.

The Greek word for **goodwill** implies that they preached for the love of preaching. Apparently, these were on friendly terms with the jailed apostle, probably ministering to his needs.

We first find the Judaizers mentioned about A.D. 49, when **certain men came down from Judea and taught the brethren, "Unless you are circumcised according to the custom of Moses, you cannot be saved"** (Acts 15:1 NKJV). The apostle Paul condemned this idea, insisting that only faith in the Lord Jesus Christ is necessary for salvation (Acts 15:1-29). In many other letters, Paul continued this same argument, insisting that believers are justified by faith alone. Becoming a new person in Christ sets one free from the requirements of the Jewish law. **It doesn't matter whether we have been circumcised or not. What counts is whether we have been transformed into a new creation** (Gal 6:15 NLT).

The history of the church reveals there has always been clergy with less than pure motives and behavior. We can look at the situation regarding certain televangelists and other clergy. History reminds us of several whose behavior did not match their message. Several of them were embarrassed; a few were imprisoned for their lack of discretion in their ministry. A Catholic priest friend of mine shared this gem, "If the church can withstand 2000 years of clergy, it can withstand anything."

It is certain that those who preached the gospel from **goodwill** comforted Paul. Paul points out that those in this group were motivated by **love**. Whether he means love of the gospel or love of Paul is not clear. It is probably a good measure of both. These had no self-serving agenda to promote and in no way gave Paul trouble. There were probably many more of these, but the former made a lot more noise.

When we consider the broad spectrum of preachers in our society, it is not hard to find those that appear to be preaching from many different motives. In their own mind, I'm sure they all feel they are people of **goodwill**, trying to preach the truth and correct errors.

Paul credited the **good will** preachers with **knowing that I am put here for the defense of the gospel**. They understood Paul's pure motives. The word **defense** comes from the Greek word *apologia* (ap-ol-og-ee'-ah). From this word, we get the biblical study called "apologetics." That is simply defined as the branch of theology that is concerned with defending or proving the truth of Christian doctrines, not apologizing for being a Christian. Paul was not in prison on a charge of murder, treason, or any other serious crime. He was there to defend his Christian beliefs, ultimately before the emperor.

Selfish ambition translates a word used in elections. It shows a desire to put oneself forward in a partisan and fractious spirit. This word is used several years earlier in Aristotle, where it denotes a politician's self-seeking pursuit of political office by unfair means. Unfortunately, one can look at American politics at election time to see a good example of this. This word describes the spirit of those who were opposed to Paul. Unfortunately, some preachers in our society seem to be motivated by some kind of religious-political agenda. This is usually to gain control of something, a church, a denomination, or perhaps a bunch of money.

Paul describes their motives by saying they wished to **stir up trouble for me while I am in chains**. This appeared to be the agenda of some of the troublemakers. I'm sure being in prison was stress enough without having agitators trying to make life even more unpleasant. But it seems to be human nature to strike someone when he is down, particularly if that downed individual is perceived as an enemy.

Motivation. What gets us going? Money drives the greedy. Materialism pushes the empty. Pleasure moves the hedonistic. Love ignites the passionate. Hatred explodes the violent. Jealousy inflames lovers. Arrogance energizes the self-centered. Hormones overwhelm the rapist. Laziness pacifies the indolent. Fantasy inflames the pornographer. Curiosity captivates the inquisitive.

In our humanity, we have all experienced the broad spectrum of human passions. Some good. Some bad. Have we not all felt hope, loving and being loved, self-confidence, well-being, joy and gladness? Who among us has not felt loneliness, fear, hate, helplessness, and the whole spectrum of human emotions? Identifying with the feelings of another often motivates us to reach out to serve. The true Christian spirit is serving because people need service. Giving because a project needs money. Caring because hurting people need care. Loving because everyone needs love. This is all done without waving a flag to get attention. Often we do it anonymously.

As Christians, we must always be concerned about our motives. And the highest motive is always to honor and serve Christ.

Here is a paraphrase of Phil. 1:15-17. **Some who do not agree with me, preach about Christ for no better reason than they are jealous of me. They see me as their rival and they want to pick a fight. There are others who preach Christ out of sincere goodwill. These want to help me. 16 They know I am not a common criminal, but I'm in jail so I can defend the Gospel. The former preach with an ulterior motive. In their insincerity, they just want to make my prison experience as miserable as they can** (DLR).

CHAPTER 6

A Lifestyle of Ultimate Trust

As the apostle sits in his prison room teaching the truth to those who visit him and the guards who constrain him, he is aware that others on the outside are teaching false doctrines with impure motives. In this passage, we see how gracefully Paul looks at this situation.

Phil 1:18-20 NIV **But what does it matter? The important thing is that in every way, whether from false motives or true, Christ is preached. And because of this I rejoice. Yes, and I will continue to rejoice, 19 for I know that through your prayers and the help given by the Spirit of Jesus Christ, what has happened to me will turn out for my deliverance. 20 I eagerly expect and hope that I will in no way be ashamed, but will have sufficient courage so that now as always Christ will be exalted in my body, whether by life or by death.**

In verse 18, Paul shows himself to be more gracious than most Christians. In his prison cell, he learns of those preaching lies. He hears that they are denouncing him and what he teaches, claiming Paul to be in error. He senses that these are ambitious people, eager to take his place of leadership when it comes to Christian teachings. They are magnifying themselves more than they are magnifying Christ. The natural response to this kind of attack is to fight back. We certainly see this in the modern world as we see people of different denominations promote their beliefs with aggression. We see leaders inside denominations battling for places of leadership and control. Each individual views his point of view as correct and his opponents as being in error.

But, Paul sees in this dissension a greater good. The name of **Christ is preached**. He was surely not happy with the errors being taught. However the fact that Christ was being preached, and His name being heard, was cause for rejoicing. Some mention of Christ is better than no talk about of Christ.

Two men in a prison Bible class despised each other. Each tried to live his newfound Christian life, but in different ways. They were housed in different dormitories. They each witnessed to others about their faith — but differently. They each read the Bible — but had different interpretations. Each attended church — but sat on different sides of the building. In Bible class you could feel the tension between them. They disagreed — disagreeably. One day after a church service, I looked back and saw them hug each other. They said to me, "We need each other. Most of the 800 men in this prison need Christ. We need to help each other in our Christian witness." Central to the teachings of the Bible is that we are to honor and respect each other. The world needs a spiritual witness, even if it comes in different ways.

Of this I rejoice reflects great nobility on the part of Paul, and nothing, perhaps, could better show his absolute love for the Savior. When ministers of our own or other denominations preach what we regard as error, and we are aware they are attracting a large following, we too can find occasion to rejoice for they preach Christ. We would much prefer that the message of Christ always be preached in truth, and from the motive of love. But the announcement of the fact that man has a Savior is a cause to rejoice. Let us always remember it is God's prerogative to judge the ministry, behavior, and motivations of others. That is not in our job description.

Paul sees the proclamation of the gospel as his ultimate **deliverance.** The Greek word for deliverance is *soteria* (so-tay-ree'-ah). This is most commonly translated "salvation." It usually refers to the saving act of Christ on the cross. In this case, it refers to deliverance from jail. It also may refer to his hope to be released from prison and see his Philippian friends again. This was Paul's **earnest expectation and hope.** We cannot imagine the apostle sitting in the corner of his room moping and complaining about his current incarceration. He is empowered by his faith in his ultimate deliverance.

We are all transients in this world. Our generation came along, and our generation will die out one day. Still, the earth will continue. As transients, we are always looking for something better. We often find something that is temporarily better. However, we are never completely satisfied.

One day, through faith, we will all come to the place for which our soul was created. We will settle down to complete satisfaction in our new home called heaven. Our transiency will end. Our journey will be complete. All the pains, worries, sadness, and struggles will be events of the past. This gives us hope. In the very midst of our deepest night, we can share Paul's **earnest expectation and hope**. The worst things that happen to us are temporary. It is going to get better.

Paul was concerned that he would **not be put to shame in anything**. He does not know what the future holds, and it is his utmost desire to handle himself respectfully and faithfully. He hopes to have strength and singleness of purpose when he faces his trial before the emperor. He looked forward to this coming opportunity to be a witness to the Gospel and the grace of God.

I have occasionally had to peek at the last chapter of a mystery novel to see how the book ended. The suspense was too overwhelming. The uncertainly too disturbing. The wait too agonizing. The possibilities too troublesome. The nights too sleepless.

Have I not used words that describe much of everyday life? Overwhelming. Disturbing. Agonizing. Troublesome. Sleepless. Why do we suffer these emotions? They all speak of an unknown future.

Studying the Bible and trusting the Author, is like peeking into the last chapter. We discover everything comes out all right. That is the way life is. The plot is unpredictable. As one proceeds through the story of life, complexities often create a seemingly senseless scenario. The Bible gives us the last chapter of life. By faith we will enter eternity with God in heaven. Knowing how the story ends, makes the difficulties and twists in the plot more bearable.

Paul wishes to have the liberty of being a witness for the rest of his life. To this end he prays for **boldness** and **courage**. Paul saw it for the glory of Christ that we should serve Him boldly and not **be ashamed** of Him. He desired freedom and liberty of mind, and without discouragement. It is equally true for us in the 21st century that, for the glory of Christ, we should serve Him **with all boldness** and not **be ashamed** of Him. Our profound faith should enable us to witness willingly. Paul was not afraid to die, and he was certain that he would be able to bear the pains and indignity of death. His body was not important at this time. The only importance was, if he were to die, people could see the sustaining power of his Christian faith. In his death, Christ would **be exalted in my body**.

Whether by life or by death, suggests these two states to be completely equal. He is completely indifferent as long as Christ is magnified in his person. For Paul, the most important thing was that he might honor the gospel. Whether he was released from prison or not, was not important. Whether he lived or died, was not important. That Christ **will be exalted** is all that mattered. I'm sure he knew if he died as a martyr, it would further the gospel. He is a role model for modern-day Christians.

Some believers come to trust Christ at an early age with little upheaval at the time. They have a growing awareness of God throughout their lives. Others come to Christ after years of rebellion and sinful living. Their newfound faith brings immediate change which continues to transform them until they die. Both experiences are valid. Neither is more authentic than the other. God and circumstances deal differently with each person. When I trusted Christ as my savior, Satan was defeated in my life. He still wins lots of battles but he lost the eternal war. Trusting Christ is a growing experience. Come celebrate with me.

Here is a paraphrase of Phil 1:18-20. **I don't care about their motives – good or bad. The important thing is that the name of Christ is being spoken in the streets. I am really happy about that. 19 I know you are praying for me because I can feel the Spirit of Christ strengthening me. One day I will be free at last. 20 I do not want to fail Christ in any way. Whether I live or die, I want people to know about the greatness of Christ** (DLR).

CHAPTER 7

A Lifestyle of Trusting in Eternity

Much is said about life and death in our world. Debates abound concerning both the beginning of life and the ending of life. In this passage, Paul looks at the relative values of living and dying.

Phil 1:21-26 TEV **For what is life? To me, it is Christ. Death, then, will bring more. 22 But if by continuing to live I can do more worthwhile work, then I am not sure which I should choose. 23 I am pulled in two directions. I want very much to leave this life and be with Christ, which is a far better thing; 24 but for your sake it is much more important that I remain alive. 25 I am sure of this, and so I know that I will stay. I will stay on with you all, to add to your progress and joy in the faith, 26 so that when I am with you again, you will have even more reason to be proud of me in your life in union with Christ Jesus.**

For what is life? The Greek word for **life** is *zao* (dzah'-o). You'll note the cognates "zoo," and "zoology." Paul was here talking about **life** and **death**. He is saying that life has no meaning apart from Christ. His life is not his own; it is completely committed to **Christ**. For him to live is for **Christ** to live also. **Life** translates a verb in the present tense. This denotes the process of continuous living, not the principle of **life** as opposed to **death**. His sole aim in **life** is to glorify Christ continuously. He will go on presenting the Gospel at every opportunity and sharing the life of **Christ** with others. **Death**, then, will bring more. If he should die, he personally, would be better off. He knew heaven was his home. We are all transients on this earth. Paul is here talking about two aspects of **life**. One is the quality of life. The other is the quantity of life. Quantity of life is measured chronologically in years and months, days perhaps hours. In recent years there's been much discussion about the question of when life begins. For centuries it was assumed that life began with the first breath and ended with the last breath. But modern scientific methods have broadened the discussion. With microscopes, sonograms, and other medical means, many have concluded that **life** begins at conception. Another theological issue that does not get much notice is the question of when the fetus receives the soul. Does that little glob of cells a few moments after conception have a soul? Or does the soul invade the fetus at some later stage of development? Theologians are divided on this issue. Of interest in this discussion is the Greek word *pneuma* (pnyoo'-mah) from which we get our English word "pneumatic." In the New Testament it is translated in various places as "wind," "breath," and "soul" or "spirit." In John 3:8 NASU, Jesus says, **The wind blows where it wishes and you hear the sound of it, but do not know where it comes from and where it is going; so is everyone who is born of the Spirit**. In this verse, **wind** and **Spirit** are the same Greek word. In like manner, "breath" and "spirit" are closely connected in the Bible. Perhaps there is still much to be discussed on this issue.

But to measure quality of life involves many other things. Quality speaks of happiness, productivity, purpose, relationships, comfort, and many other measures that we might use to decide whether life is worthwhile. We often assume that life is always better than death. Paul was not saying that here. In fact, in some ways, in some circumstances, **death** is better than **life**. This is not to say that Paul was choosing **death** at this time. It certainly could be a consideration. Terribly wounded men on a battlefield sometimes ask their buddies to kill them. Some do. They cite the Golden Rule as their justification for shooting a buddy. If they were in that condition, they would prefer to die. Such mercy killings are called "euthanasia." This word come from the Greek *eu,* "good," and *thanatos,* "death." Some deaths are better than others. We attend the funeral of a person who lingered with a long and painful illness. People say, "He's better off now." We hear a nursing home patient say, "I wish I could die and get it over with." Here is faith that life in the next world will be better than it is in this world.

Several years ago I saw a movie entitled *Whose Life Is It Anyway?* The story was of a quadriplegic who wanted to die rather than live with the limitations placed upon him. He raised the question, "Who has the right to determine whether an individual lives or dies."

One part of the question of euthanasia is, does anybody have the right to take the life of another individual even if they request it. Another part of the question is, does anybody have a right to keep people alive who don't want to be kept alive? Paul was dealing with this issue in a particular sense. He was talking about his own life or death and the value to him in either case. He was not talking about taking his own life.

In verse 22, Paul says, if he goes on living he will have **worthwhile work** ahead of him. The term **worthwhile work** is used in the sense of winning converts and furthering the spread of the gospel. It is generally agreed among commentators that the **if** clause used here is not conditional in meaning. Paul assumes that he will be free after his trial. But if he dies, his martyrdom will be a witness. He does not know which he would **choose** if the choice were his.

Verses 23 and 24 described his ambivalence. He is **pulled in two directions**. He faces two great values: one is living *for* Christ on earth; the other is living *with* Christ in heaven. The latter would certainly be his choice. He would be finished with all the trials and hardships of this earth. It is **far better** to be in heaven than any place on Earth. But there is another side, that is the need for him to continue proclaiming the message of Christ. This, he views as a need for the Philippian Christians and for the rest of the world. For Paul, this is a win-win situation. Either he wins the opportunity to continue sharing the message of Christ or he wins by inheriting his eternal reward. Paul's hypothetical choice was not between good and evil. It was a choice between two goods. We note in verse 25 that Paul had confidence that God will allow him to live on this earth for a while longer. He said, **I am sure of this**. This was in fact the case for, after having been two years in bonds at Rome, he was released. His return to Philippi would serve two purposes. He would continue spreading and defending the Gospel. This would result particularly in the spiritual growth of the Philippian Christians. **Progress and joy** share one article, so they should probably be taken closely together with **faith**. The word **faith** here stands for experience based on believing in God and trusting in Christ as Savior. For Paul, **joy** is an indispensable component of that experience. **I will stay**

on with you all. Paul had great confidence in God's providence. He knew it would be best for him to remain alive and again visit the Philippians. The purpose of his future visit would be **to add to your progress and joy in the faith**. It would be a great joy for them to be reunited. That reunion would assist them in their growth in the faith. All **joy** is truly in Christ. **Reason to be proud of me in your life in union with Christ Jesus.** In the original Greek, this is a confusing statement. It is not clear whether the pride should be in Paul or in Christ. Some translations try to bring both together. Note this one: **And when I come to you again, you will have even more reason to take pride in Christ Jesus because of what he is doing through me** (Phil 1:26 NLT). This clarifies that we are to have our pride in Jesus Christ not in any person. We started off with the question, "What is life?" And we have seen that life is far more than just a length of time. Life has a quality about it. That quality of life finds its highest measure in a relationship with Jesus Christ. No person can find more important work than finding and doing the will of Christ.

Here is a paraphrase of Phil 1:21-26. **For me to live is for Christ to live. But to die means going to heaven. I am really ambivalent. I want to do what is best for me, that is to go on to heaven. But I really need to stick around on earth to help you in your spiritual growth. Knowing you need me, I am sure I will stay alive and help you on your spiritual journey. When I come to you, we will rejoice together because of how God takes care of us** (DLR).

CHAPTER 8

㇐ Lifestyle of Persistence

On June 4, 1989, America's TV screens flashed an unforgettable image. American journalists were in Beijing to cover a peace conference between China and Russia. Mikhail Gorbachev's presence soon took a back seat to Chinese students and workers peacefully protesting government oppression and calling for more freedom. The cameras then showed more than a hundred thousand protesters in Tiananmen Square. Many were killed or injured by those controlling the crowd. Most of the world saw a lone student defying a tank in the middle of the street. Can you not see it now? The young man in a white tee shirt stands firm as a huge military tank rolls to a halt in front of him, refusing to go any farther.

Think about that one lone and defiant young man, face-to-face against a tank, that horrible machine of destruction that could easily have crushed him. That scene represents the power of ideas over physical force. This young man took a stand for what he believed. The power of an idea is stronger than tanks and guns and bullets. The apostle writes about standing firm in our belief.

Phil 1:27-30 NRSV **Only, live your life in a manner worthy of the gospel of Christ, so that, whether I come and see you or am absent and hear about you, I will know that you are standing firm in one spirit, striving side by side with one mind for the faith of the gospel, 28 and are in no way intimidated by your opponents. For them this is evidence of their destruction, but of your salvation. And this is God's doing. 29 For he has graciously granted you the privilege not only of believing in Christ, but of suffering for him as well — 30 since you are having the same struggle that you saw I had and now hear that I still have.**

Verses 27-30 constitute one sentence in Greek. Long sentences are difficult to understand so, most translations break it into several sentences to make it more easily understood.

Live your life in a manner worthy of the gospel is a rather common way to translate the first part of this passage. It is a way of generalizing what the Greek says specifically. The NLT recognizes the Greek word *polites* (pol-ee'-tace) in verse 27. **Above all, you must live as citizens of heaven, conducting yourselves in a manner worthy of the Good News about Christ**. A good translation would be "be sure and live as good citizens." *Polites* is properly translated "to live as a citizen; to conduct oneself according to the laws and customs of a state."

As Christians, we recognize that we are citizens of two kingdoms: we are citizens of some country here on earth. But, we are also citizens of the kingdom of heaven. But this passage does not indicate which of these kingdoms this citizenship is talking about. The Amplified Bible translates it this way, **Only be sure as citizens so to conduct yourselves [that] your manner of life [will be] worthy of the good news (the Gospel) of Christ**. You'll discover most other translations generalize the matter, suggesting we live with Christian conduct.

The Christian looks at life as a citizen of two worlds. Yes, our feet are firmly planted on this earth. On this planet we have all the hardships, pains, and sufferings that afflicts humanity. Often we can do little about them. We are also citizens of another world. By faith, we are a part of the Kingdom of Heaven. This gives us another view. We see things in an eternal context.

God looks down on our distress and says, "I see the *big picture*. You can't see it from down there." The big picture includes *forever*. As a Christian I need often to remind myself that I have one foot on earth and the other in heaven.

Paul was proud of his Roman citizenship. He may have been suggesting that his readers be faithful **citizens** of this Roman city, Philippi. However, he may have implied our citizenship in the kingdom of God. In either case, his readers should live above reproach. They should live their lives **in a manner worthy of the gospel of Christ.**

Whether I come and see you or am absent and hear about you suggests the outcome is not certain. Paul may or may not see them again. Either way it will be okay, because Paul knows they are supporting him and fighting Satan with him.

Striving side by side ... for the faith of the gospel. *Sunathleo* (soon-ath-leh'-o) pictures the idea of "striving together" as in an athletic contest. It is from this Greek word that the English word "athletics" is derived. Not that Paul and the Philippians are in competition with each other, rather, they are members of the same team. Together they are to fight against the enemies of the Gospel. **Striving side by side** is literally "in one spirit." This speaks of the united purpose of the Philippian Christians. Their purpose is the same as Paul's. What high compliment!

Phil 1:28. **Are in no way intimidated by your opponents.** The word for **intimidated** is more literally, to be "terrified." There are times and places where the persecution of Christians is so atrocious that they may well be terrified. **Evidence of their destruction** translates a word, that suggests the lost condition of the nonbeliever. Paul is suggesting that the Christian's bravery will show the lost their willingness to suffer for Christ. If Christians are willing to suffer for Christ, their faith must be genuine.

In verse 29, we see the Christian **privilege** having two prongs: the first is the privilege of **believing in Christ** for our salvation and everyday sustenance. It is a privilege to believe in Christ, because it is by faith in Christ that our sins are forgiven, that we become reconciled to God, and have the promise of heaven.

The second prong is the privilege **of suffering for him.** Suffering for Christ certainly sounds strange in 21st-century America, though common in some other parts of the world. It is certainly not thought of as a **privilege**. Yet this sentiment frequently occurs in the New Testament. Consider what is said of the apostles, that **they departed from the presence of the council, rejoicing that they were counted worthy to suffer shame for his name** (Acts 5:41 KJV). Also consider 1 Peter 4:13 KJV, **But rejoice, inasmuch as ye are partakers of Christ's sufferings.** In the New Testament it is seen as a privilege to suffer for the cause of Christ.

31

Suffering for Christ is considered an honor, because it is only His most faithful servants that He thus honors. **Blessed are you when men shall persecute you ... for great is your reward in heaven** (Matt 5:11-12 KJV). Both **believing** and **suffering** are present infinitives in Greek. This verb tense indicates that the privilege of believing Christ and suffering for Him is not a once for all action but is continuous. Let us also consider the fact that the only suffering that really counts is suffering for the advancement of the cause of Christ.

Verse 30. The Greek of this verse is somewhat obscure. It means literally "having the same conflict such as you saw in me, and now hear in me." The participle "having" agrees with "you" of the previous verse; so "you" is the logical subject of the participial clause. The emphasis is on the word "same," and several translations make this fact explicit: **Now you can take part with me in the battle. It is the same battle you saw me fighting in the past, and as you hear, the one I am fighting still** (TEV). Paul is here emphasizing the fact that we Christians are in the same battle together. With Christ on our side we are assured of victory.

Here is a paraphrase of 1:27-30. **Now, live your life in a manner that is worthy of your citizenship in heaven; in so doing you will promote the good news about Jesus Christ, and I will know that you are standing firm in your belief. I know that you are striving side by side with me to promote the Gospel. Do not be intimidated by your opponents, they will destroy themselves while you are growing in your faith. This is the way God works; He gives us the privilege of believing in Him as well as privilege of suffering for Him. We both share in this struggle.**

CHAPTER 9

ᚪ Lifestyle of Wise Choices

Within most adults is a deep, spiritual longing for a fulfilling life. We can find fulfillment in a right relationship with God. We can serve Him with the strength we have. Every Christian is called of God.

One may be called:

First to be a Christian — then a plumber.

First a Christian — then a carpenter.

First a Christian — then a homemaker.

First a Christian — then a teacher.

First a Christian — then a minister.

The primary call is to follow and imitate Christ. When we have a healthy relationship with Christ, we find life fulfilling.

Phil 2:1-4 TEV **Your life in Christ makes you strong, and his love comforts you. You have fellowship with the Spirit, and you have kindness and compassion for one another. 2 I urge you, then, to make me completely happy by having the same thoughts, sharing the same love, and being one in soul and mind. 3 Don't do anything from selfish ambition or from a cheap desire to boast, but be humble toward one another, always considering others better than yourselves. 4 And look out for one another's interests, not just for your own.**

Note the KJV for comparison. **If there be therefore any consolation in Christ**. Most commentaries indicate that the Greek conjunction *ei* ("if" in several translations) does not express doubt. The TEV leaves out that word altogether. Rather, it assumes the conditions to be true. **Your life in Christ makes you strong**. Paul uses four conditions in this verse, relying on that assumption. What does a person get out of following Christ? The apostle Paul names four things:

Strong. The translators seem to have a field day with this particular noun. The Greek is *paraklesis (par-ak'-lay-sis) meaning* "something put down alongside." We find the following words used to translate it: "comfort," KJV; "encouragement," NIV; "cheering each other up," TLB; "strength" NCV. It pictures the believer walking side by side with Christ and gathering His strength in the process.

Comfort. We find a similarity between strength and comfort. The English word comes from two Latin words: *Com* means "with," and *fortis* means "strength." Thus, "comfort" means, "with strength." We have comfort when we have strength with others and within ourselves. II Cor.1:4 says, **He comforts us in all our troubles so that we can comfort others** (NLT).

Fellowship usually translates *koinonia* (koy-nohn-ee'-ah). In this verse **fellowship** is linked with **Christ**. There is a oneness between the Christian and the Spirit of Christ. This verse gives a word picture of the Christian walking hand in hand with the Spirit of God.

Kindness and compassion. The KJV translates this "bowels and mercies." You'll recall we dealt with this in 1:8. The message is that as brothers and sisters in Christ, we treat each other with heartfelt tenderness. Remember the golden rule, **Do to others what you would have them do to you** (Matt 7:12 NIV).

The power to minister to wayward spiritual siblings is the power to accept people "as they are." All people share common ground. In my ministry as a Prison Chaplain, I have listened to inmates' stories of anger, violence, bitterness, helplessness, and hurt. I have listened as they recounted times of harming other people. I have empathetically experienced torment and pain with them. We have laughed with each other. We have wept together. Their eyes have met mine as we broke bread from the same loaf, shared the same cup, and praised the same God. Together, we prayed and read the Scriptures. We sat side by side in spiritual retreats. We worshiped in the same assembly. I've patted them on the back, hugged and encouraged them.

Sometimes, we may consider wayward souls as too far gone. We isolate others because we have not genuinely appreciated what Christ has done for us. We forget *our* past. We forget *our* humanity. We forget what Christ rescued *us* from. May I never forget my sinful past and my human weaknesses when working with other people.

In verse 2, Paul is calling for church unity. He speaks of having the **same thoughts, sharing the same love**. He wants all Christians to be of the same mind, to love each other, and to agree in all things. The Greek word here is *sumpsuchos* (soom'-psoo-khos). It is a combination *sun* "with" and *psuchee* "Spirit." It pictures, a group who is harmonious in soul or spirit. They are in tune with Christ and with each other. Paul says if his readers have this kind of harmony, he will be happy.

Verse 3 is a call to humility. No doubt Paul had seen his share of pride in Rome. His enemies boasted of their superior theology and presented themselves as important people. This **selfish ambition** has already appeared in Phil 1:17. It describes a desire to do things for selfish purposes which result in creating a partisan spirit. It describes a person who will use political tactics to get what he wants for himself. **A cheap desire to boast** translates a single Greek noun, which means "vainglory" or "self-deceit."

Not long after the terrorist attack on the World Trade Center, the news media showed scenes of life in Afghanistan under Taliban rule. They showed a man with a steel rod publically whipping one of his four wives. The newscaster explained that she had allowed a part of her face to show in public. I wondered how women could tolerate such dominance by their husbands.

Then I recalled that many Christian denominations place wives in a submissive role in the Christian home and limit roles they can fulfill in the church. Many Christian women go along with that, also.

Fundamentalism – be it Jewish, Palestinian, Political, Islamic, or Christian – always leads to the same place – *arrogance*. "I am right and everyone who disagrees with me is wrong!" is the dominant theme of fundamentalism. For the fundamentalist of any faith or philosophy or politics, there is no room on this planet for anyone who disagrees with them. In philosophy, the fundamentalist Taliban and the fundamentalist Christian are not too far apart. It is a matter of degree – not of kind. The Christian should rise above this kind of self-righteousness in all his relationships.

The final phrase of verse 3 defines to **be humble. Always considering others better than yourselves**. Oh my! That is a hard one. It means simply that I am never to think that I'm better than anyone else. Paul is attacking a basic part of human nature. We tend to think, "I am right, others are wrong." "I do it the right way, but others do it wrong." "My theology is better than anyone else's." "If people would only listen to me, everything would be all right."

How do I handle this when I compare myself with the drunkard, the thief, the murderer, the rapist? Do I consider myself better than those reprobates? Here's something to work on.

Verse 4 tells us **And look out for one another's interests, not just for your own**. This is a value system contrary to our basic human nature. By nature we are self-centered, and look out for ourselves. In Christ we are to be transformed and highly considerate of other people. We are to rejoice in the prosperity of others as truly as in our own.

In one's theology, childhood experiences influence lifelong choices. Some hold beliefs their parents or preacher uncle or grandparent held. These ancestors taught them to "hold to the truth!" Others were taught to "think for your self!" Still others heard, "Don't go to extremes in anything!" You can see how conservatism, liberalism, or moderation would fit these influential childhood injunctions. Lord, give us wisdom in our everyday choices.

Here is a paraphrase of Phil. 2:1-4. **Has your life in Christ changed you in any way? Has His love made you strong and does His love comfort you? Your fellowship with His Spirit will give you kindness and compassion toward each other. You will make me really happy if you agree with each other wholehearted and work together with one mind and purpose. Completely set aside any selfish ambition and boasting. Rather, consider yourselves servants of each other. Always consider others as being more important than yourself. Don't just look out for your own good, but consider the needs of others as well** (DLR).

A Lifestyle of Service

Phil 2:5- 7 NASU Have this attitude in yourselves which was also in Christ Jesus, 6 who, although He existed in the form of God, did not regard equality with God a thing to be grasped, 7 but emptied Himself, taking the form of a bond-servant, and being made in the likeness of men.

Verse 5 is the introduction to a hymn that is included in verses 6-11. This verse tells us that we are to have the same pattern of thinking that Christ had. Then the hymn tells us what that pattern of thinking is, the essence of humility. The verb *phroneo* (fron-eh'-o) **attitude** is in the present tense, and is plural. The present tense shows that this is supposed to be continuous action. We are always to be humble. Being plural, tells us this is for the entire congregation. A loose translation of this verse could be, **all of you should keep on thinking and behaving like Christ thinks and behaves** (DLR).

Paul has already introduced the idea of humility in verse 3, **but in humility consider others better than yourselves** (NIV). Now he is going to expand the concept of humility using Christ as the supreme example. The point here is, Christ left a state of inexpressible glory, and took upon Himself the most humble form of humanity, and performed as a servant, that He might benefit us.

Verse 6 begins the poem or hymn describing the ultimate humility of Christ. **Who, although He existed in the form of God, did not regard equality with God a thing to be grasped**. The first part of the phrase describes the Son of God in his state before becoming a man. The important phrase is *morphe* (mor-fay') *theos* (theh'-os). *Morfee* is translated "form." *Theos* is the Greek word for "God." Combined they referred to the essential attributes as shown in the **form of God**. This clearly refers to the Son of God in His heavenly home, in His preincarnate state, possessing all the attributes of God. This is a clear statement by Paul of the deity of Christ. We can only guess at what the Son of God was like before His incarnation. He certainly possessed all the majesty and glory of the eternal God. The word *harpagmos* (har-pag-mos') which is translated **grasped** in the NASU, implies a thing eagerly to be seized, coveted, or desired. So, His being equal with God was something the Son of God had, but not something to be kept to Himself. The phrase **did not regard** means "did not consider." The Son of God did not deliberate the matter of coming to Earth. He saw His mission of redemption as outweighing any heavenly pleasures or status He might desire to hold onto. The sense is, "He did not hang onto His exalted glory," as a person does who holds firmly to his possessions. Here are two other translations: **Though he was God, he did not think of equality with God as something to cling to** (NLT). **Who, being in the form of God, thought it not robbery to be equal with God** (KJV). The essence of this verse is that the preincarnate Son of God enjoyed all the glory and power of the eternal God. Let us look briefly at the word *incarnate. Carne* is of Latin origin and refers to flesh. So the biblical word "incarnate" means "in the flesh." In recognizing His eternal destiny, Christ would become flesh to fulfill His eternal purpose. Verse 7 continues the transition from Son of God in heaven to Son of God on earth. **But emptied Himself, taking the form of a bond-servant, and being made in the likeness of men.**

The Greek for **emptied** is *kenoo* (ken-oo), "to empty." This has given rise to what is called the "kenotic" theory of incarnation. He gave up His heavenly privileges and status to become human. The Son of God emptied Himself into the person of Jesus Christ. *Eugene Peterson* translates it this way, **When the time came, he set aside the privileges of deity and took on the status of a slave, became human!** (MSG). The word *ekenoosen,* "emptied Himself," does not occur elsewhere else in the New Testament. The idea is that of bringing about emptiness or nothingness. In this case, Christ lays aside His rank and dignity, and He assumes a humble rank and position. We must not say He literally stripped Himself of His divine nature and perfection, that would be impossible. Even as a human, He carried with Him the divine attributes of God. After fulfilling His purpose on earth, He would return to heaven and His former position of glory. His journey to earth was a temporary assignment. God became human because of his infinite love for mankind.

In America we think of love as a feeling. A young man feels a surge of affection and passion in his soul toward a young lady and says, "I love you!" A grandmother feels the warmth and joy of a child cuddling in her lap and says to the lad, "I love you!" A child gets a bicycle for Christmas and says, "I love it!" Another says, "I would love to go to England and France." The Biblical sense of love is more than feeling. 1 Cor 13 describes love as action. Words like patience, kindness, humility, giving, purity, and believing, are descriptions of love in that chapter. They all talk about how we behave.

Early in my prison ministry, I talked with a young man who became uncontrollably angry at his eight-month-old son's crying. He snatched him from his crib and threw him against the wall, killing the child. How could I love such a person? I learned to love the person but not the behavior. There were times I did not like certain inmates. I did not *like* the gruff, the irreverent, the selfish, or those who preyed on others. But I could *love* them. I could patiently listen to their troubles. I could help them adjust to the difficult circumstances of prison. I could believe in their capacity for change. When Christ emptied himself and became human, he was expressing love in action.

The status of a slave translates the Greek *morfeen* (mor'-feen) *doulou* (doo'-lou).We saw this word *morfeen* in Phil 2:6 where it is said He had **form of God**. This pairing, pictures Him the **form of God** in heaven, and the **form of a bond-servant** (NASU) on earth. In our poem, we see these two as parallel expressions of the nature of the Son of God. This distinguishes the different forms held by the Son of God. The word **servant** translates the Greek *doulou*. We looked at this word in Phil 1:1. The apostle's purpose is to state the depth of humiliation to which Christ descended. In the New Testament world, there was no position lower than that of a bond slave.

Became human. The King James and some other translations suggest **made in the likeness of men**. Likeness suggests similarity, but this does not mean that Christ's humanity is unreal, as the Docetics believed. It is important to note that the Son of God in the person of Jesus Christ became one of us. The Docetics held that Jesus only had the appearance of a body. They reasoned, that all human flesh was sinful and therefore a perfect God could not inhabit human flesh. To the Docetics, the human nature of Christ and the incidents of His earthly career were nothing more than an illusion. The apostle John identified these Docetics with the Antichrist (1 John 2:22-23; 4:2-3) and extended special effort to speak of the humanity of Christ (1 John 1:1-3).

Jesus was of Hebrew parentage. He grew up in a Jewish home. We assume He learned the Jewish tradition and memorized much of the Old Testament, as all Hebrew boys did. He grew up observing the Passover as a memorial of God's deliverance from Egyptian slavery. He remembered His history.

It was important to Jesus that we, too, remember our spiritual history. As He grew up remembering through the Passover, He established a way for us to remember — through the Lord's supper. Breaking bread symbolizes the painful, broken life He suffered for us. The juice or wine represents His blood shed for our salvation.

Through Christ's birth, God Himself entered the stream of humanity. Through His death and resurrection, He paid the ultimate price for our eternal salvation. We stand in awe of God's majesty when we remember all His goodness. Christ gave the perfect example of Christian service. He gave His life for the good of others. He should be our supreme model.

Here is a paraphrase of Phil. 2:5-7. **Every Christian should keep on thinking and behaving like Christ thinks and behaves. God, Himself, knew He should not hold on to His majestic status. That would be selfish. He gave it all up to become human. In fact, He became so low, it was like becoming a bond-slave** (DLR).

₰ Lifestyle of Humility

Phil 2:8-9 AMP And after He had appeared in human form, He abased and humbled Himself [still further] and carried His obedience to the extreme of death, even the death of the cross! 9 Therefore it's [because He stooped so low] God has highly exalted Him and has freely bestowed on Him the name that is above every name.

Let's look briefly at a time line. Up to this point, we find the Son of God in heaven and the process of His becoming human. At this point, we see what happened after He became human. This is expressed in the phrase **after He had appeared in human form**. We find the humbling process was not completed in His merely becoming human, but it continued all His life as a human being. This is expressed in the phrase **He abased and humbled Himself [still further]**. Let's try picturing it this way. We find the Son of God in heaven holding a cup in His hand. In the cup are all of His attributes: majesty, deity, omnipotence, omniscience, omnipresence, complete love, righteous judgment, glory, splendor, holiness, worthy of worship, worthy of praise. We then see the eternal Son of God take this cup and lock it away in a safe, to be taken again later.

Down on Earth is a baby who holds a cup. He fills it with all the attributes of a human – poverty, humanity, wisdom, pain, sorrow, humility, criticism, hatred, and false accusations. It was this last content that caused Him to pray in the garden, **My Father, if it is possible, may this cup be taken from me. Yet not as I will, but as you will** (Matt 26:39b NIV).

The word order in Greek, suggests these differences: in Phil 2:7, we have **[He] emptied Himself,** with the emphasis on the person; whereas here we have **[He] humbled himself**, with the emphasis on the act. We see the Son of God transferred from the very throne of God to the lowest position on earth – a babe in a manger. One would think that when the Son of God became a man, He should have been a prince or a king, and appeared in majesty. But quite the contrary: He took upon Himself the form of a servant.

Sometimes it is difficult for us to grasp His human nature. We are told too little about it. We can only wonder and suppose. I suppose when He was growing up, He exasperated His mother, Mary. It is likely He and John the Baptist had their share of wrestling matches. He probably did all the things normal Jewish boys did: played games with other children; memorized Scripture; studied the law of Moses; attended Jewish school; learned the proper Jewish diet, and learned a trade.

Let's look at Him as a young carpenter. When He hit His thumb with a hammer, did He say, "Lordy, Lordy!" Or did He say, "Me! Me!" Here are a few things I know He did not do. He did not endanger the lives of several other people by getting in the driver's seat of an automobile with His blood-alcohol level above the limit. He did not send a text message while driving at a high speed down a populated road. He did not rush through the signal light as it turned red just to save a few minutes.

We certainly note how times have changed. A first-century drunken Jew on a donkey, going home from a party is no threat to people around. At least a donkey is in control and knows what he's doing and probably knows the way home. An intoxicated 21st-century partygoer in a Cadillac is a threat to everyone in his vicinity. Neither he nor the Cadillac is in control.

And carried His obedience to the extreme of death. This phrase defines the extent of Christ's humility. It is this kind of humility that is urged upon the Philippian Christians, and consequently on the Christians of all ages. This emptying oneself on the part of the Son of God was a voluntary humiliation. This is why Paul presses the example of Christ upon the Philippians. This is the supreme example of renunciation. The point of this expression is this: one may readily and cheerfully obey another where there is no particular peril, however, the likelihood of danger puts our obedience in a different light. Consider the soldier, who volunteers to go into a battle that is almost certain to end in his death, saving the lives of his friends. This illustrates what Christ did for us.

Let us look at the word "excruciating." Webster defines it as "something extremely painful; causing intense suffering; unbearably distressing; torturing: an excruciating noise; excruciating pain." It describes the worst possible pain. "Excruciating" comes from two Latin words *ex* "out of" and *cruc* "the cross." Here we see where Christ's suffering sets the standard for intense pain.

Verse 9. **Therefore [because He stooped so low]**. The Amplified Bible adds the brackets to explain what **therefore** refers to. This verse marks the turning point in the eternal drama. Two contrasts are seen in the change: (1) exaltation vs. degradation, and (2) Lord vs. servant. Up to now we see the humility and obedience of Christ. But now God takes the initiative in bestowing on Christ the highest honor in existence.

Because of what Christ did, **God has highly exalted Him**. This is where we should shout, "Hallelujah!" The Greek language suggests "God hyperexalted Him." This is a rare compound verb occurring only here in the New Testament. This is language in the superlative. The contrast is between the lowest point of His earthly role (servant-obedience-criminal death) to the highest heavenly honor and position. We do not know what all this includes. Though it seems, in His resurrection, He returned to an even higher position than His preincarnate state. What could this higher state be? What glory could He have after the ascension that He did not have before His incarnation? One suggestion is that now He is both Son of Man and Son of God.

And has freely bestowed on Him the name that is above every name. This is an aspect of His being **highly exalted**.

That means Christ has been given a name that **is above every name**. Verse 10 suggests that name is the personal name, **Jesus**. Whatever the name, it is clear it designates unparalleled dignity and honor. He again sits on the throne of glory, and possesses universal dominion. The resurrected Jesus deserves from all mankind reverence of the highest kind. Verses 11 and 12 will discuss our appropriate response.

How different from the arrogance of other powerful leaders of His day. Consider the Caesars, they created for our western calendar an abnormality: Sept is the prefix for *seven*. September is the *ninth* month; Oct is the prefix for *eight*. October is the *tenth* month; *Nov* is the prefix for *nine*. November is the *eleventh* month; *Dec* is the prefix for *ten*. December is the *twelfth* month.

As best I understand it, for several years before Christ, the Roman calendar had ten thirty-six day months. That led to a heat wave in January and snow in June. Newer calculations demanded 365 days. In his arrogance, Julius Caesar decided that since they were revising the calendar anyway, there should be a month named after him. Thus, for their safety, they obeyed the king's command and inserted July after June. Not to be outdone, Augustus Caesar also claimed a month for himself. So, August was also added.

Does this appear egotistical? Yes. We may observe that people in power tend to become arrogant. It matters little whether the power comes from a civil or religious position or wealth or guns and ammunition. Power wants to be noticed. Jesus said, **People who are humble will be happier in the end, because they will inherit heaven** (Matthew 5:3 DLR).

Here is a paraphrase of Phil 2:8-9. **After he came to earth in human form He kept on humbling Himself by serving others rather than Himself. His obedience to God took Him all the way to death – the excruciating death on the cross. But, because He humbled Himself to such a degrading state, God has highly exalted Him and has given Him the highest name possible** (DLR).

CHAPTER 12
ᛖ Lifestyle of Devotion

Phil 2:10-11 KJV **That at the name of Jesus every knee should bow, of things in heaven, and things in earth, and things under the earth; 11 And that every tongue should confess that Jesus Christ is Lord, to the glory of God the Father.**

Most translations follow the KJV rather closely in this passage. A few minor variations will be pointed out as we go through.

That at the name of Jesus every knee should bow. *En* is the Greek word for **at**. It can also be translated "in." Nearly all translations maintained the **at**. The meaning in this passage is that Jesus rightly deserves the honor that is properly due only to God. **The name of Jesus** appears to be the highest honor that can possibly be bestowed as suggested in verse 9. The bowing of the knee (literally or figuratively) properly expresses homage, respect, and adoration. The phrase **every knee should** bow is an idiomatic expression referring to reverence and esteem of the worshiped object. This is recognition of His majesty and power. Bowing of the knee sometimes refers to prayer. The TEV makes the meaning explicit and translates verse 10 **And so, in honor of the name of Jesus all beings in heaven, on earth, and in the world below will fall on their knees.** That is, all people should adore him. Having risen from the grave, it is proper that all **in heaven** and **on earth** should worship Christ. And that the time would come when He would be thus everywhere acknowledged as Lord. That occasion will come for every individual, either while we live here on earth or face God in the judgment.

Verse 10. **Of things in heaven, and things in earth, and things under the earth**. Paul now describes the enormous

45

universal power and authority of Jesus Christ. In the Greek there are three adjectives which here function as nouns. The KJV understands the adjectives to be neuter, and translate them as **things**. It is more rational to interpret the reference as relating to rational beings. **So at the name of Jesus everyone will bow down, those in heaven, on earth, and under the earth** (CEV). It is likely that **those in heaven** refers to heavenly spirits, angels, and perhaps those who have already died and gone to heaven. **Those on earth** refers to people living at the present time. This expresses their need to make a decision for Christ. And **those under the earth** refers to those in the realm of the dead. The Greek word for this is found only in this place in the New Testament. But some years earlier, Homer used it as an adjective for departed souls, those who were buried, and for the dead. This is sometimes referred to as Hades or Sheol.

In ancient times, people believed there was an underworld where the spirits of the dead carried on an obscure existence. In any case, the author intends to show that the Lordship of Jesus Christ is celestial and universal. Some believe **under the earth** refers to those who have, through their own fault, died without having received God's salvation. According to this view, even the lost will bow before Him. They will be forced to yield in unwilling reverence to Jesus Christ who died for their salvation. Having rejected Him will not excuse them from this eternal humbling experience. It is too late to accept His salvation, but they must acknowledge Him as Lord of the universe. This phrase is doubtless intended to show the universality of the adoration-worthiness of the risen Son of God. This does not imply that the lost will have a second chance. This will not be a confession unto salvation; this will be a confession of acknowledgment. They may be forced to say simply, "I was wrong. Jesus is Lord, after all."

Verse 11. **And that every tongue should confess that Jesus Christ is Lord, to the glory of God the Father**. In verse 10, we had **every knee**. Here in verse 11, we have **every tongue**. Not only do we acknowledge His lordship in bodily actions, but also in confession of faith. In the phrase, **Jesus Christ is Lord**, we have one of the earliest confessions of faith.

This is a simple statement regarding what Jesus Christ is to the Christian community. **Lord** was the most common title applied to Jesus by the early church. The Septuagint uses the word **Lord** to translate the Hebrew "Yahweh." Yahweh is a form of the verb "I am." It is the personal name of God and suggests His eternal nature. We find this first introduced when Moses is on the mountaintop viewing the burning bush. **Moses said to God, "Suppose I go to the Israelites and say to them, 'The God of your fathers has sent me to you,' and they ask me, 'What is his name?' Then what shall I tell them?" 14 God said to Moses, "I AM WHO I AM. This is what you are to say to the Israelites: 'I AM has sent me to you'"** (Ex 3:13-14 NIV).

Lord is also used in the general sense of "master" or "sir." When it is applied to Jesus, it has a unique significance. When Jesus Christ is celebrated as Lord, He is put in the place which rightly belongs to God alone. This recognizes that Jesus Christ has dominion over the entire universe.

The ultimate purpose in giving honor to Jesus Christ, and in acknowledging Him as Lord, is to make a declaration **to the glory of God the Father**. This is another way of saying "so that all will praise God." We looked at the word **glory** in Phil 1:11. With these words, the hymn which began in Phil 2:6 draws to an appropriate close. The authority of the Son is derived from the Father. Only God the Father has the ultimate sovereignty but He has given it to, and shares it equally with, His Son.

The question here raised for every individual is not whether or not we will acknowledge Jesus as Lord. The question is, when will we acknowledge Jesus as Lord? While we live on earth? Or after we die? That is a question facing every human being.

Notice the words here, **everyone will bow down ... every tongue will acknowledge**. This does not look like the 21st century does it? In our world today, we have many who do believe that Jesus Christ is God's son and the Savior of the world. We have many others on the other extreme who do not believe and actively and openly attack Christianity as phony and built upon lies. And then it appears the majority is somewhere in between. They neither declare themselves to be Christian nor non-Christian.

But, according to the Bible the story is not over. There is a judgment day to come. On this great day every person will be asked the question, "What did you do with Jesus Christ?" Did you kneel before Him and confess your faith in Him? Did you recognize Him as the Lord of your life and live for Him day by day? Or, did you ignore or reject Him?

Jesus is the most important and most noble name ever spoken on the face of the earth. Christians should share that name proudly and unashamedly.

When a person goes to buy a car, house, stereo, or a CD player, the sales person may say, "The bottom line is — you pay so much today and so much each month for so many months and it is yours." The "bottom line" describes a condition one must meet to gain something from another.

For centuries people have been asking what one must do to go to heaven, "What is the bottom line?" When I stand at the great judgment throne of God, I want Him to forget the wrongs that I have done. Through the death of Christ on the cross, He forgave all my sins. I also want Him to forget whatever good I may have done. He must not mistake any good deeds as my hope of salvation. He wants my eternal life to be a gift.

All I ask of God is to remember me as loving Him. This is deep theology. This is a simple statement of what God's grace is all about. **For by grace are ye saved through faith; and that not of yourselves: it is the gift of God: 9 Not of works, lest any man should boast** (Eph 2:8-9 KJV).

Here is a paraphrase of Phil 2:10-11. **At the name of Jesus every one will one day bow down, all of the Angels, and Saints who have died, those who still live on earth, and others in the world below. Every tongue will acknowledge that Jesus Christ is the Eternal Lord, thereby glorifying God the Father** (DLR).

ᴀ Lifestyle of Determination

Phil 2:12-13 TEV **So then, dear friends, as you always obeyed me when I was with you, it is even more important that you obey me now while I am away from you. Keep on working with fear and trembling to complete your salvation, 13 because God is always at work in you to make you willing and able to obey his own purpose.**

Verses 12 and 13 represent one long sentence in Greek. For the sake of clarity several translations break it into two sentences. Verse 13 is assurance that God is working to fulfill His purpose in our lives. It is God's purpose for us to do our part in bringing about maturity in His family. **God** is in an emphatic position in the Greek text. This indicates the importance of God in this discussion.

Paul calls his readers **dear friends**. This again reinforces his affection for the Philippian Christians. He is calling upon them to **obey** his instructions. He is not here correcting them for any past negligence. He notes that **you always obeyed me when I was with you**. When he was with them, they were all obedient. That was important. Paul was a good teacher and he taught the truth well. So, it was important that they follow. The apostle is here giving some positive affirmation.

Paul then says, **it is even more important that you obey me now while I am away from you**. It is not clear exactly why Paul made this distinction between their obedience while he was there and while he was away from them. But he is challenging them to continue to act on the same principles and from the same motives and having the same temperament found in Christ. They were to be industrious in promoting His glory. The Philippians had always shown great respect to the apostle, and followed his teaching. He commends them for this and appeals to them to continue in obedience. Paul may have sensed it would be more difficult for them to follow his teachings without his physical presence to encourage them.

The last half of verse 12 has been subject to many different interpretations. In the KJV it reads **work out your own salvation with fear and trembling**. Some people interpret this as an indication of "works salvation." That is, we must do good works in order to earn our salvation. Paul always speaks of personal salvation as an act of God, a gift from God provided through Christ's death on the cross. And that to **work out your own salvation** (KJV) suggests our need for continued growth in our Christian life. The Greek word for **salvation** is *soteria* (so-tay-ree'-ah). This is a noun which has as its root meaning "to rescue." It is, in various places, translated in the KJV as "deliver," "health," "salvation," "save, "and "saving."

It appears Paul is telling the Philippians that they are to be faithful in their Christian life. I will share some other translations at this point. **Work out (cultivate, carry out to the goal, and fully complete) your own salvation** (AMP). **Work hard to show the results of your salvation** (NLT). **Keep on working to complete your salvation** (NCV). **So work with fear and trembling to discover what it really means to be saved** (CEV). **To complete your salvation** (TEV). In each of these we get the sense of striving to the finish. This exhortation assumes a human free agency in carrying on the work of one's salvation. In no way does it suggest our earning salvation through human effort. After one paints a car, he uses a buffer to **work out** the rough surface and produce a shine. When one plants a garden, all summer long he **works** his garden to get rid of the weeds. When one pours a concrete walk, he uses a trowel and **works out** the rough spots to produce a smooth surface. When one receives God's salvation, he spends the rest of his life **working out** the imperfections in his life. The Greek word clearly means "work on to the finish."

The challenge for us is to continue walking in the same faith, and serving in the same way, until the whole scenario of our salvation is completed. Our goal is to be filled with love for God and humanity. We are to walk without blame in our daily lives, and to bear fruit that will lead us to a full Christian character. We do this to the end goal of showing the effects of our everlasting life. Just as our bodies depend on continual sustenance and measures to maintain health, so our spirit needs constant attention. This topic denies the idea that once we are saved we need not be concerned about our Christian lives and we can indulge ourselves any way we wish. Our profession of faith is just the beginning of a lifelong process of fulfilling our salvation.

The Bible looks at salvation in three tenses: past, present, and future. When a person believes in Christ, he is saved from the penalty of sin (Acts 16:31). As we live our daily lives, we are in the process of being saved from the power of sin (Eph 1:13-14). Our ultimate goal is being saved from the very presence of sin (Titus 2:12-14). We obtained this final goal when we reach heaven. Our salvation will be complete when Christ returns, and the kingdom of God is fully revealed (Matt 13:41-43). The Philippian Christians are encouraged to work toward this goal with **fear and trembling**. This is a typical Old Testament expression suggesting humility, reverence and devotion to God. This is a wholesome respect for the need to do right. Working out our salvation to completion is not an easy task. We are to consider the seriousness of it along with its difficulty. None of us want to come up short in that great judgment day. The Greek word for **fear** is *phobos* (fob'-os). It is from this Greek root that we get all of our modern words for the phobias: Friday the 13th – Paraskavedekatriaphobia; open spaces – Agoraphobia; Corpses – Necrophobia. You get the picture. There are thousands of phobias.

Keep on working is a present participle, indicating the action is to be continuous. This appears to imply that we are to further the work of God in the Christian community. This does not suggest primarily physical activity. Rather, it speaks of willingness to serve. **To make you willing and able to obey his own purpose** expresses the reason God is at work in us. The NLT translates this part of verse 13, **For God is working in you, giving you the desire and the power to do what pleases him**. The KJV puts it this way, **For it is God which worketh in you both to will and to do of his good pleasure**. In all these translations, we see that our desires, as well as our works are for the purpose of pleasing God. The word **pleasure** translates the Greek *eudokia* (yoo-dok-ee'-ah); which includes the ideas of satisfaction, delight, kindness, purpose. Pleasing God should be the Christian's primary goal. **Willing** here is certainly more than mere "wishing." It involves resolve to carry out the purpose of God. In these verses, we find that God is **working in** the Christian. We also find the Christian is supposed to be at work in the world. But ultimately, God does

51

it all. He does His part. Then we are to do our part. Both the "will" and the "doing" have their source in God.

Most twenty-first-century Americans have bought into the world's notion of success. They measure success in promotions in one's career, a good income, and respect in the community. Outward symbols of success are a beautiful house, two or three impressive cars, a boat or jet skis, a recreational vehicle, children in a prestigious college. A bumper sticker summarizes this philosophy, "Life is a big game. He who dies with the most toys — wins." Others have reminded us that even "he with the most toys" also dies.

Even Christians who plan to do something for God may get sidetracked by personal agendas. God's people need to understand that those who live by God's wisdom and obey His commands have achieved success already. Believers have a different definition of success than non-believers. Jesus said it this way, **First, go after God's kingdom, then you'll have everything else you need** (Matthew 6:33 DLR).

Here is a paraphrase of Phil 2:12-13. **Therefore, my dear friends, as you have always followed my suggestions when I was with you, continue that even in my absence. Bring to full completion the process of salvation planted in you. Do so with reverence, awe, and serious contemplation. You cannot do this in your own strength because it is God working in you to bring about pleasure and satisfaction for Himself** (DLR).

CHAPTER 14

ᚫ Lifestyle of Joy

Phil 2:14-18 CEV **Do everything without grumbling or arguing. 15 Then you will be the pure and innocent children of God. You live among people who are crooked and evil, but you must not do anything that they can say is wrong. Try to shine as lights among the people of this world, 16 as you hold firmly to the message that gives life. Then on the day when Christ returns, I can take pride in you. I can also know that my work and efforts were not useless. 17 Your faith in the Lord and your service are like a sacrifice offered to him. And my own blood may have to be poured out with the sacrifice. If this happens, I will be glad and rejoice with you. 18 In the same way, you should be glad and rejoice with me.**

Phil 2:14. **Do everything without grumbling or arguing**. That sounds like my mother talking, probably every mother talking. I'm not saying that in a grumbling way, just making an observation. In the Greek, verses 14-16 consists of one complex sentence, but for clarity of thought most modern translations break it into several short sentences.

In these verses, Paul continues his orders by pointing out specific patterns of behavior that are not acceptable for Christians. Most commentators assume he does not refer to **grumbling** against God. Rather, they are complaining among each other. Both nouns are plural in the Greek although most translations find it easier to put them in the singular. The Greek word for **grumbling** is *goggusmos* (gong-goos-mos'). This is onomatopoeia. If you say the word slowly and with a soft voice, you will sense that the Greek word itself sounds a bit like **grumbling**. It is also translated "murmuring." The Greek word translated **arguing** is *dialogismos* (dee-al-og-is-mos'). You can readily see our English word "dialogue" in it. The root idea is "to deliberate." Thus, the word can be used in either a positive or negative sense. In various places, the KJV translates this word "dispute," "doubting," "imagination," "reasoning," "thought." This surely means that Paul charges them to do all things in a quiet and peaceful manner. There are to be no brawls or open, loud arguments. You will recall in Phil 2:3-5, Paul spoke of the need for humbleness of mind and considering others better than themselves. In that way, the spirit of God might work among His people in a diplomatic way. This is important because the light of truth, and practicing the Christian life, are often lost in the heat and passion of arguments.

Then you will be the pure and innocent children of God. By avoiding **grumbling or arguing** within the Christian community, the Philippians are to become **pure and innocent**. The adjective **innocent** is often used to describe someone who has a very good reputation. Other people find little fault with the faithful's daily living. **Pure** means literally "unmixed" or "unadulterated." In Bible times, it was used of wine not mixed with water and of metal that contained no alloy. **Children of God** is a rather common New Testament phrase that describes the relationship between God and believers.

Paul points out the difference between the children of God and the people in the community around them. Does not this **crooked and evil** statement describe much of our world today? We can spend lots of time talking about how bad the world is, however, it has been this way for centuries; perhaps, this century is no better or worse than any other. The word for **crooked** means to distort, to twist, to turn to one side. Lost people of the world have always had distorted ways. This passage is a clear indication that Christians are not to be like them. Our lives are to be so pure and so above reproach that we will **shine as lights** among them. That is a big order.

YLT translates **shine as lights** this way, **among whom ye do appear as luminaries in the world**. Most translations change **appear** to **shine**. Whether this is to be taken as indicative or imperative, is equally debated. But the context appears to demand the imperative. The imperative implies a duty. The Greek noun rendered **luminaries** is frequently used to refer to the heavenly bodies, the sun, the moon, and the stars. Some commentaries suggest this is an allusion to a lighthouse that was placed on a dangerous coast. The purpose is to warn approaching vessels of danger and save them from shipwreck.

In like manner, the light of Christian testimony shines in a dark world to rescue people from the dangers in each person's spiritual journey.

Among the people of this world. The Greek word *kosmos* (kos'-mos) is usually translated "world." It refers to the "world order" as in "cosmic." This includes the physical earth and all its inhabitants. It is to these inhabitants that the Christians are to share the light of the world that brings eternal and abundant life.

As you hold firmly to the message that gives life. This is the only occurrence in which Paul uses the phrase the **message that gives life**. In the Greek this is literally, **the word of life** (NIV). This challenge is given to every believer. We are all to shine as lights in the world by sharing the **word of life**.

Then on the day when Christ returns, this is the same as the day of judgment. It is called the **day of Christ** (KJV) because Christ will be the celebrated object which will be acclaimed on that day; it will be the day in which He will be recognized as the judge and king of all the world.

I can take pride in you (CEV). **That I may rejoice** (KJV). This pride or rejoicing was the result of the Philippian Christians letting their light shine. It was through Paul that these Philippians had become Christians. It was through Paul that they had a church.

I can also know that my work and efforts were not useless. Paul is here looking back over his Christian life. As he views his converts living the Christian life and spreading the gospel, he sees his ministry has been fulfilling. The KJV more accurately reflects the Greek **that I have not run in vain**. This metaphor pictures an athlete dashing toward the finish line. Paul says he did not run for nothing. The King James uses the phrase **neither have I laboured** in vain. The Greek word implies working to the point of weariness or exhaustion.

In verse 17, the scene shifts from the athletic stadium to the altar and sacrificial rites. **Your faith in the Lord and your service are like a sacrifice offered to him**. The noun rendered **service** is the Greek word *leitourgia* (li-toorg-ee'-ah). You can see therein the English cognate "liturgy." In common usage, it meant a service to the public or the state, like a civil servant. In the New Testament it is more often used in reference to priestly functions, especially the offering of sacrifices in the Temple.

This next section becomes a bit more complicated. **And my own blood may have to be poured out with the sacrifice**. **Poured out** translates the Greek word *spendo* (spen'-do) "to pour out as a libation or a drink offering." The drink offering was usually a cup of wine poured out on the ground to honor a deity. This phrase suggests the idea of devoting one's life or blood as a **sacrifice**. Paul is talking about the possibility of his martyrdom, that he might have to be sacrificed.

If this happens, I will be glad and rejoice with you. The possibility of death does not cause Paul any grief, but rather joy. Paul is confident that for him death will be a gain. In his death, Christ will be glorified and the gospel proclaimed. Notice how often Paul refers to rejoicing. In Christ he has joy and he wants to share it with all the Philippians. It is clear that Paul is not afraid of death. It will be a way of furthering the gospel.

Verse 18. **In the same way, you should be glad and rejoice with me**. In this verse the Philippian Christians are called upon to be happy about their sacrifice and to share their joy with the apostle. Just as Paul has had to sacrifice, so must the Philippians sacrifice. But also, just as Paul finds joy in his Christian life of service, so should the Philippians enjoy in their life and service. They should rejoice together.

Here is a paraphrase of Phil 2:14-18. **Do everything without grumbling, faultfinding, and arguing among yourselves. Let people see you as innocent and pure. Let no one point a finger of blame at you. You live among wicked and perverse people. Let them see you as bright lights illuminating this dark world. Offer everyone the message of eternal life. That will give me reason to be proud of you when Christ returns. That will show I have not run this race in vain. It may be that I may have to pour out my blood as a sacrifice to God, just as your service is a sacrifice. If that happens we should all be joyful together** (DLR).

CHAPTER 15

𝔸 Lifestyle of Teamwork

Phil 2:19-24 NLT If the Lord Jesus is willing, I hope to send Timothy to you soon for a visit. Then he can cheer me up by telling me how you are getting along. 20 I have no one else like Timothy, who genuinely cares about your welfare. 21 All the others care only for themselves and not for what matters to Jesus Christ. 22 But you know how Timothy has proved himself. Like a son with his father, he has served with me in preaching the Good News. 23 I hope to send him to you just as soon as I find out what is going to happen to me here. 24 And I have confidence from the Lord that I myself will come to see you soon.

The apostle Paul plans to send this letter with Epaphroditus. That would probably happen within a few days. He also hopes to send Timothy to Philippi, perhaps at a later date, so he may remain in Philippi for a while and be a help to the Philippian Christians. Timothy would then return with a report about the Philippians.

In saying, **If the Lord Jesus is willing**, Paul is expressing his confidence that God is in his plan. The timing of this journey for Timothy is given only as **soon**. He apparently did not send him with Epaphroditus because he still needed Timothy's service in Rome.

The purpose of Timothy's returned to Philippi is stated as **he can cheer me up by telling me how you are getting along**. It is obvious that this will be a short-term visit. Timothy will go to Philippi and encourage the church there. He will also learn how they are getting along, and take that message back to Paul. Paul has a lot of emotional investment in the Philippian Christian family. He is eager to know how they are getting along. **Cheer me up** translates *eupsucheo* (yoo-psoo-kheh'-o), meaning literally "be well in the soul." This word was common in gravestone inscriptions, representing a pious wish for the dead: "Farewell." or "Be it Well with Your Soul." Perhaps the modern equivalent of "Rest in Peace."

We first find **Timothy** in Acts 16:1. Paul found him in Derbe and Lystra and arranged for Timothy to join him on his journey. He continued with Paul to Troas where Paul felt the call to go to Macedonia. In Macedonia he went to Philippi. No mention is made of Timothy being with Paul at Philippi. But after he left that city we find Timothy was with him in Berea. We can only conclude that Timothy was with Paul and Silas in Philippi also. So, Timothy would be returning to a group of people he already knew.

Verse 20. **I have no one else like Timothy, who genuinely cares about your welfare**. There were others Paul could send, but none had the concern that Timothy had. Paul considered Timothy as a son, and Paul's sending him on such an occasion would support the feelings of a father who should send a dearly loved son on an important journey.

No one else like translates a word used nowhere else in the New Testament. The Greek word describes a sharing of intimate feelings. It is literally "of the same soul." Paul is here expressing how close is his bond with Timothy.

Paul wants his friends in Philippi to know that Timothy is one who **cares about your welfare**. Both Timothy and Paul have friends in Philippi. Both had a share in the founding of that church. Paul emphasizes that his concern is genuine and sincere, saying that Timothy is a person he can rely on to carry an accurate message to the Philippians.

The Greek word translated **genuinely cares** comes from an early root word that means "legitimate" as a legitimate birth. There is no phoniness in his caring.

All the others care only for themselves. What is Paul referring to here? Is he talking about the general state of the Christian world around him? Or is he making a harsh and sweeping condemnation of his local Christian friends? Or is he just in a pessimistic mood? It is clear that Timothy is the only one he could count on at that time. It appears everyone else was concerned about his or her selfish interest. The Greek literally says "all seek after their own thing." This must include the persons who preached Christ of envy and strife spoken of in Phil 1:15. Even those who preached the Gospel out of good will might not be fit for such an assignment as this. It would take special dedication and zeal to endure the distance and the dangers along the way. **And not for what matters to Jesus Christ**. Literally this is, **the things of Jesus Christ** (MSG). I wonder if this could be said of a large segment of Christians in every age. We should not be too harsh in our judgment. It is not easy for one to leave one's business and the comforts of home, to take the message to some remote part of the world, or even next door in some cases. There is a shortage of self-denial in every age. We may look at ourselves and see how we measure up.

Verse 22. **But you know how Timothy has proved himself. Like a son with his father, he has served with me in preaching the Good News**. Now we are back to Timothy. Paul's affection for him and confidence in him is obvious. **Timothy has proved himself**. This verbal phrase is the translation of a Greek noun *dokime* (dok-ee-may') meaning literally "proof." It is related to the verb used in Phil 1:10, where it is used to test gold or silver for its quality. Timothy passed the test. He is also of great value to the Philippians. This makes him the perfect one to take this journey on behalf of Paul. The fact that the Philippians **know how Timothy has proved himself** is evidence that Timothy was with Paul at Philippi.

Like a son focuses on the very close alliance in which the two worked together for the spread of the gospel. **Has served** involves the Greek word *douleuo* (dool-yoo'-o); a form of *doulos* popping up again. They have worked like "slaves" in spreading the gospel. We may interpret this phrase as an explanation of how Timothy proved his worth. Let us note Christians are not servants *to* one another, but serve God together *with* one another.

Down through my years as a minister, I have had a close relationship with several young ministers. With some, we were members of the same church. Others were college students doing intern assignments at the correctional center. Some were students in Clinical Pastoral Education. These were always meaningful relationships. I am proud to see their achievements and believe I had some part in their spiritual growth. In some measure, I feel they are my spiritual children. Many pastors experience this kind of closeness with some young disciple.

I hope to send him to you just as soon as I find out what is going to happen to me here. Paul is here explaining why he is not sending Timothy at this time. **What is going to happen to me** surely refers to the verdict of the trial. At this time he apparently did not know whether he would be convicted or not. He expected the verdict to be handed down in the near future. He continued to be in captivity. Assuming an acquittal, he would feel free to send Timothy on his journey. If, on the other hand, he was condemned and put to death, he would then have no further need for his services. Either way, the timing of Timothy's journey depended upon the trial.

And I have confidence from the Lord that I myself will come to see you soon. The verb used for **I have confidence** is a strong verb. It shows confidence, reliance, and hope. But we notice the limiting factor **from the Lord**. This phrase carries with it the force of what in today's Christian conversation we would normally say, "If it is the Lord's will." It is only with faith in the Lord that Paul can look forward with confidence. This is not used in a perfunctory way. Paul's whole life seeks to fulfill the will of Christ.

Here is a paraphrase of Phil 2:19-24. **If it is the Lord's will, I hope to send Timothy to you soon. When he returns, he can cheer me up with good news about you. There is no one else who, like me, cares as much about your welfare. Most of the people here are concerned about their own affairs, not the affairs of Jesus. I don't need to tell you how Timothy has proved his worth. You already know that. You also know that he is like a son to me. We are a real father-son team working together to spread the gospel. I am waiting until I know how my trial is going to turn out before I send him to you. I think everything is going to be okay, and I also will be able to come visit you soon** (DLR).

CHAPTER 16

₳ Lifestyle of Trust

Phil 2:25-30 NLT **Meanwhile, I thought I should send Epaphroditus back to you. He is a true brother, co-worker, and fellow soldier. And he was your messenger to help me in my need. 26 I am sending him because he has been longing to see you, and he was very distressed that you heard he was ill. 27 And he certainly was ill; in fact, he almost died. But God had mercy on him—and also on me, so that I would not have one sorrow after another. 28 So I am all the more anxious to send him back to you, for I know you will be glad to see him, and then I will not be so worried about you. 29 Welcome him with Christian love and with great joy, and give him the honor that people like him deserve. 30 For he risked his life for the work of Christ, and he was at the point of death while doing for me what you couldn't do from far away.**

Philippians is the only book in which we find **Epaphroditus**. Can you imagine why any mother would give her son a name like that? We don't hear that name in 21st-century America. But, she had a reason. Place your finger over the first two letters of his name, and you will see his name is derived from Aphrodite (Venus), the goddess of love and beauty. Thus his name would mean something like "Handsome," "Loving," or "Charming." It is likely his mother was a pagan living in the Greek city of Philippi. Along with several other gods, she likely worshiped the Goddess, Aphrodite. The one thing we remember about Aphrodite is thousands of prostitutes lived at her Temple. Men worship Aphrodite by connecting with her prostitutes.

Philippi was a city in northeastern Greece, a city of some importance in the Roman province of Macedonia. It was in the middle of rich agricultural plains and near the gold deposits of Mount Pangaeus. It was, in Paul's day, a Roman city with a Greek-Macedonian population and a small group of Jews.

Originally founded in the sixth century B.C. as Krenides by the Thracians, the town was taken over after 360 B.C. by Philip II of Macedon, the father of Alexander the Great, and was renamed for himself, "Philip's City." It was conquered by Rome in 42 B.C.

Epaphroditus was a member of the church there. The church at Philippi sent Epaphroditus to visit Paul. The purpose of his visit was to take a gift to him. Paul commends Epaphroditus very highly saying that **He is a true brother, co-worker, and fellow soldier**. Epaphroditus was still with Paul as this letter was being written and he would bear it on his journey back to Philippi. In this, we get the picture of Paul and Epaphroditus working side by side in defending the gospel together. We are here reminded that Christianity involves warfare; conflict with Satan and his cohorts is inevitable. Our daily battles are the evil works that Satan produces.

And he was your messenger to help me in my need. In this we see that Epaphroditus was sent to Paul specifically to be a help to him, ministering to him and his everyday needs. That would likely include running errands for Paul while he was in prison. The word **for messenger** is *apostolos* (ap-os'-tol-os) "one who is sent." This word is usually reserved for the original apostles. However, this is not to imply that Epaphroditus has that status. **Helped me in my need** translates leitourgos (li-toorg-os') which is used for the ritualistic functions in the Temple. It is from this word we get our English word "liturgy." In the Jewish religion that would include keeping knives sharp, cleaning up blood after a sacrifice, burning residue, removing ashes, burning incense, lighting candles, extinguishing candles, and a hundred other ritualistic jobs that were performed each time a sacrifice was made. Many branches of Christianity have their liturgies as well.

I am sending him back to you. Apparently, he had accomplished much for the apostle Paul. But now, **he has been longing to see you**. He is apparently homesick.

He was very distressed that you heard he was ill. Apparently Epaphroditus had been seriously ill. It distressed him that the church back at Philippi had heard about that. He may have been one of those who preferred to suffer alone without too much empathy from others. In verse 27, we see how sick Epaphroditus was, **He almost died.** But, God healed him. That spared Paul from having **one sorrow after another**. The Greek is "sorrow upon sorrow." Paul has the sorrow of his imprisonment and all the discomforts that accompany that. He was delivered from the discomfort of having Epaphroditus die. There is no indication this healing was a miracle performed by Paul. Such miracles seem to be reserved for times when divine intervention would further the Gospel.

Verse 28. Because of Epaphroditus' homesickness and his recuperation from his illness, Paul was **more anxious** to have him return to Philippi. Paul is also stressing that the Philippians will be glad to see Epaphroditus. With Epaphroditus being in Philippi, Paul will **not be so worried about** the Philippians.

The Christian can live a life of trust, trust that God will care for their needs. Most can enjoy life. We want to wake up in the morning having had a good night's rest. We want to have pleasant encounters with others during the day and a happy family. One ingredient in happiness is a healthy love of self.

When we love ourselves we consider eternal values and claim the promise of eternal life. We seek forgiveness from the Eternal God. Loving ourselves means taking care of ourselves and avoiding self-destruction, be it slow or rapid.

Is it wrong to love ourselves? Not at all. It is *very right,* if that love develops our relationship with God. When Jesus said, **Love your neighbor the way you love yourself** (Matthew 22:39 DLR), He vindicated self-love. Not to the point of egomania. Not to arrogance. Not to self-centeredness. Not to conceit or self-glory. Rather, we recognize our worth in relationship to God and His purpose on earth. He declared us worthy. He found us worthy of His sacrifice on the cross for our forgiveness. God loved us that much. We should love ourselves.

Welcome him with Christian love and with great joy seems to be an unnecessary statement, in the light of their love for him. **Give him the honor that people like him deserve**. This is a reminder that Christians are to honor those who do good work for Christ. We are not to take any honor away from Christ Himself, but to recognize the good service of the faithful. Sometimes Christian leaders make a point of trying to get honor for their various services. That is not done in the Christian spirit. That does not describe **Epaphroditus**. Rather, he should receive honor at the suggestion Paul.

Verse 30. One of the reasons Epaphroditus was worthy of honor was that **he risked his life for the work of Christ**. The word **risked** is one used in gambling. It pictures Epaphroditus, in the midst of his illness, risking his life to work for Christ. In all of this, Epaphroditus was **doing for me what you couldn't do from far away**. The people in Philippi were unable to help Paul across the miles, so Epaphroditus filled the gap and did for Paul what the Philippians would like to have done. This is not a complaint by the apostle suggesting negligence on the part of the Philippian church. This is something like our giving money for foreign missions. We are unable to be on the field with missionaries, but we can send money to support them.

Here is a paraphrase of 2:25-30. **I believe it is now time to send Epaphroditus back to you. He has been a very faithful laborer and soldier in the battle for truth. He has served you well in the way he has taken care of me. He was very upset when he learned about your concern for him in his illness. There was good reason to be concerned. He almost died. God healed him and he is now becoming homesick. He misses you so much. God rescued me also by delivering me from the added sorrow if Epaphroditus had died. I am more than willing to send him to you because I know you will be happy to see him, and I won't have to worry about you any longer. Celebrate his homecoming and give him the honor a faithful servant deserves. He risked his life doing for me the things you could not do because of the distance between us** (DLR).

CHAPTER 17

ꓯ Lifestyle of Christian Freedom

Christian freedom does not suggest we can do anything we
want to with abandon, and still maintain a Christian witness,
we are expected to have a lifestyle that shows we love Jesus. In
this lesson, we will see that outward acts do not gain us a
relationship with Christ. It is what happens on the inside that
counts. Let's read what the apostle says about this.

Phil 3:1-6 NKJV **Finally, my brethren, rejoice in the Lord.
For me to write the same things to you is not tedious, but
for you it is safe. 2 Beware of dogs, beware of evil workers,
beware of the mutilation! 3 For we are the circumcision,
who worship God in the Spirit, rejoice in Christ Jesus, and
have no confidence in the flesh, 4 though I also might
have confidence in the flesh. If anyone else thinks he may
have confidence in the flesh, I more so: 5 circumcised the
eighth day, of the stock of Israel, of the tribe of Benjamin,
a Hebrew of the Hebrews; concerning the law, a Pharisee; 6
concerning zeal, persecuting the church; concerning the
righteousness which is in the law, blameless.**

Finally. At this point, Paul appears to be concluding his letter.
He suddenly decides to remind his readers of some very
important things. He feels the need to add a few words of
warning against his opponents of whom he has already
written.

This change of emphasis is quite abrupt. In Phil 3:2, Paul
erupts into warnings against false teachers, **those dogs**, who
threaten to impose on the Philippians the burdens of the
Mosaic law, including **circumcision**. The section that follows,
Phil 3:2-21, is a vigorous attack on these Judaizers (cf. Gal
2:11-3:29) or Jewish Christian teachers. This gives us insight
into Paul's own life story and into the doctrine of justification,
the Christian life, and ultimate hope.

Rejoice in the Lord. This points out the idea that Christians are to be filled with joy. The reason for our joy is rooted in our relationship with Jesus Christ. He has saved us and He sustains us. The Greek word for **rejoice** is also used as a greeting, as in "Godspeed." The Greek word for **Lord** is *kurios.* (koo'-ree-os). We looked at that word in 1:14.

For me to write the same things to you is not tedious is literally "to write the same things to you is not irksome to me." Paul is here repeating some things he had spoken or written in the past saying, **I don't mind repeating what I have written before** (TEV). This is most likely an introduction to what follows in 3:2 ff. Paul feels free to warn the Philippians a second time. This is a repetition of the warnings against false teachers which the apostle has stated in other letters. This may make their Christian lives a bit more **safe**. **Safe** means primarily "stable," and is used of something to be relied on as helpful.

If all four chapters were originally a unity, then one must assume that a break occurred between the writing of Phil 3:1 and Phil 3:2, possibly involving the receipt of bad news from Philippi, or perhaps a nights unrest, or some disturbing news from outside regarding the Judaizers. At least it appears Paul had some reasons for delaying his words of thanks for the aid brought by Epaphroditus till the end of his letter. He again felt the need to attack the legalists of his day.

Some have suggested that this abrupt change indicates that the letter consists of two or more fragments which have been put together. Up to four fragments have been suggested. However, there is no need to assume the existence of several separate letters. Some suggest Paul was probably dictating the letter (possibly to Timothy or Epaphroditus), when news reached him of the threat from enemies of the gospel reaching Philippi, hence Paul's warning. There were two threats: from outside the church – the Judaizers (3:2-4:1), and from inside the church – Euodia and Syntyche (4:2).

The harsh language of 3:2 is followed by Paul resuming his very personal tone at 3:4, which is similar to the rest of the letter. Paul's close relationship with the Philippians shows in chapter three, just as in the first two chapters. The letter almost certainly forms a unit, not being written at different times, although the great hymn of Christ (2:6-11) could be a quotation of a well-known hymn of the time.

Paul begins his list of warnings. In Greek the imperative **beware** is repeated three times in this verse. This clearly emphasizes the earnestness and seriousness of the warnings. **Beware,** or "be on your guard against" **of dogs. Dogs** were regarded by the Jews as low-down and contemptible creatures, being unclean animals in the Old Testament law. They are usually mentioned with disdain in the Old Testament. This is the most insulting term of abuse often used by orthodox Jews regarding the Gentiles. Here Paul turns it around and applies this term to those Jewish Christians who pervert the gospel and undermine the principles of the faith, by demanding good deeds as necessary to obtain salvation.

Beware of evil workers. The Greek word for **evil** is *kakos* (kak-os'). It carries the idea of worthless, depraved, or injurious. Several English words from this root began with "caco." "Cacophony" refers to a bad sound. This writer suffers from "cacography" or illegible handwriting.

Beware of the mutilation! The word used for **mutilation** is *katatome* (kat-at-om-ay'). This is a compound word joining *kata* (down, or off) and *temno* (to cut), thus "to cut off." Paul is here sarcastically saying the Judaizers are engaging in **mutilation** (as in cutting off the penis).

For **circumcision**, he uses the word *peritome* (per-it-om-ay'). This is a compound word joining *peri* (around) and *temno* (to cut), thus "to cut around" (as in cutting around the foreskin).

Paul uses this distinction here in a contemptuous fashion to draw a distinction between the ritualistic **circumcision** of the Jews and the true **circumcision** of the heart experienced by Christians. Paul is likely here referring to the same Judaizers he spoke of in 1:17. Here Paul draws the clear distinction between the outward motions of a ritualistic religion and the true inward change of heart through a personal relationship with Christ.

Verse 3. **For we are the circumcision, who worship God in the Spirit, rejoice in Christ Jesus, and have no confidence in the flesh**. Here, Paul is summarizing the nature of the true relationship with Christ. Several translations use the word "true" to describe **circumcision** in this passage. The TEV translates **no confidence in the flesh** as **we do not put any trust in external ceremonies**.

Verse 4. **Though I also might have confidence in the flesh**. Note the shift here to the word **I**. This makes it clear that what follows is Paul's personal testimony. It is designed to place him in the position of an authentic Jew. His authenticity gives him the right to warn them in such blunt terms.

I more so can be translated **I have greater reason for trusting in myself** (NCV). Paul is saying he has every right to brag about his being a sincere Jew. However, all of these external things are of no value in the great matter of salvation, even so, he enumerates them.

Verse 5. **Circumcised the eighth day**. According to Genesis 17:14, male children were to be **circumcised** on the eighth day. Paul claims that in his case his situation rightly fulfilled the law. Paul notes that he is **of the stock of Israel**. The word for **stock** is *genos* (ghen'-os) meaning "kin." Our English word "genealogy" comes from this Greek root. Paul was not circumcised as an adult proselyte. He claims he was a descendent of the patriarch **Israel**, or Jacob. Therefore, he could trace his genealogy as far back as Abraham himself, and then to Adam.

Of the tribe of Benjamin. The tribe of Benjamin was regarded with special esteem because it had given the nation its first lawful king. That King's name was Saul, the same as the apostle's original Hebrew name.

A Hebrew of the Hebrews. Although Paul was born in a foreign country, Tarsus, both of his parents were Hebrews. There was no mixture of Gentile blood, and they maintained their Hebrew speaking traditions. Jewish people who lived outside of Palestine and spoke Greek were called Hellenists. Paul's family retained their Hebrew identity in all matters. Due to the nature of the New Testament world, Paul probably knew Hebrew, a language used primarily in the Scriptures and temple worship, and spoke Aramaic (the common street language of the Jews), Greek, and Latin.

In these last claims, Paul enumerates the identity he has inherited. What follows is this statement about what he accomplished personally as a Jew. **Concerning the law, a Pharisee**. The Pharisees made up the strictest sect among the Jews. They took upon themselves the sacred duty of keeping and defending both the Mosaic Law and the tradition of the fathers which were designed to interpret the law. Those traditions degraded into hundreds of petty rules and regulations faithful Jews were expected to keep. In this, Paul was boasting of his faithfulness to the Jewish religion. Being a **Pharisee** was a matter of pride. Today we tend to look at the negative side of being a **Pharisee**. Paul was looking at the positive side. Some people use the word "Christian" in a derogatory manner. We Christians find it a source of pride.

Verse 6. **Concerning zeal, persecuting the church**. For a Jew, to be zealous for his religion was of the highest importance, as it is with some Christian groups who put high value on "soul winners" or "prayer warriors." Paul points to his persecution of the church as strong evidence of his zeal of the Jewish faith. The term **zeal** is *zelos* (dzay'-los) meaning "heat." The term **church** in this passage likely refers to the local congregations he persecuted. The word for church is *ekklesia* (ek-klay-see'-ah) "a calling out." Thus it is used for any group of people, especially a religious congregation, assembly, or church. Let us remember Paul was the prime mover in the persecution and death of Stephen. This **zeal against the church** continued until his conversion, then it became **zeal** for the church.

Concerning the righteousness which is in the law, blameless. It was believed by the Jews, especially the Pharisees, that salvation can be earned by keeping the law and the traditions of the fathers. Paul now speaks of his legal uprightness as one of his greatest personal achievements. Paul claims that, before his conversion, he had done everything required to accomplish salvation according to that legalistic plan. The adjective rendered **blameless** is the same word translated **innocent** in Phil 2:15. The word is often used to describe someone in whom others people find no fault. Paul is claiming that, as a devout Pharisee, he met all the standards of righteousness prescribed by the Law.

In the verses that follow, Paul points out how fruitless this is. And that anyone relying upon these external accomplishments will be found lacking in the day of judgment. All of this is to show the difference between Paul's beliefs and those of the Judaizers who continually attacked him. Paul has established that he is a more faithful Jew than any of them, yet he relies only on Christ for salvation.

The lesson here is that anyone who is relying upon his good works or his exemplary life as his ticket into heaven will find

69

that his ticket is counterfeit. He must have faith in Christ and accept Him as personal savior. True Christians are not those who put on a good outward show, but those who have an inward transformation by the power of God.

Here is a paraphrase of Phil 3:1-6. **Finally, my brothers and sisters, be happy you know the Lord. I am going to repeat some things about which I have said and written on other occasions. This will be a safeguard for you. Watch out for those dogs who mutilate the body. We, who believe in Christ, are the true circumcision. We true believers worship in the spirit of God and express our belief in Jesus Christ. We put no confidence in the flesh. If anyone thinks good works will save him, let him look at my credentials. I was circumcised on the eighth day. I am a pure-blooded Hebrew of the tribe of Benjamin. And I kept the law as meticulously as anyone could. I was a Pharisee so zealous that I persecuted the church. No one could point an accusing finger at me. I was without fault** (DLR).

CHAPTER 18

ℳ Lifestyle of Self-Denial

What is of value to you? House, car, bank account, health, comfort, your education, your Sunday School perfect attendance pins, your piety – shall I go on? Let's look at value through the eyes of Paul.

Phil 3:7-11 HCSB But everything that was a gain to me, I have considered to be a loss because of Christ. 8 More than that, I also consider everything to be a loss in view of the surpassing value of knowing Christ Jesus my Lord. Because of Him I have suffered the loss of all things and consider them filth, so that I may gain Christ 9 and be found in Him, not having a righteousness of my own from the law, but one that is through faith in Christ—the righteousness from God based on faith. 10 [My goal] is to know Him and the power of His resurrection and the fellowship of His sufferings, being conformed to His death, 11 assuming that I will somehow reach the resurrection from among the dead.

But everything that was a gain to me. In verses 5-6, Paul enumerated all the advantages of his birth, his education, and how he meticulously kept the Jewish law. He is suggesting here that he formerly believed all of these things could be a great advantage in a matter of earning salvation. He highly valued all the matters concerning his moral integrity and his religious conformity. The word for **gain** is plural in the Greek, perhaps reflecting his enumeration of several items.

Paul is saying that what he once counted as great profit he now sees as a total loss. After his conversion, he has a complete change of perspective saying, **I have considered [all] to be a loss**. The Greek word for **loss** implies a "hindrance" or an "injury." Paul actually looked upon those

71

former advantages as obstacles to his findings salvation in Christ. He had to unlearn all of those concepts of being saved by works when he experienced salvation by grace. Often, people of good morals and good reputation are the most difficult to lead to Christ. They think they are good enough.

Because of Christ. On the road to Damascus, Paul experienced an absolute transformation (Acts 9:1-19). No longer was salvation a matter of doing great things. It became a matter of knowing a great person. In the 21st century, over much of the world, there continues to be the concept that if we do enough good things we will earn our way into everlasting life. The gospel dispels that idea completely, telling us that our salvation depends upon our belief in Jesus Christ.

Eugene Peterson translates this verse: **The very credentials these people are waving around as something special, I'm tearing up and throwing out with the trash — along with everything else I used to take credit for. And why? Because of Christ**.

Verses 8-11 is one long and complicated sentence in the Greek. Many translations restructure it into a series of shorter sentences to make more sense in English. **More than that**, Paul uses five disjointed, and somewhat confusing, particles to introduce the statement that follows. You will find these translated in several different ways, all of which are designed to show the force and passion of his conviction regarding the supremacy of faith in Christ. A few examples follow: **Yea doubtless** (KJV), **What is more** (NIV), **Not only those things** (TEV), **More than that** (NASU). In each of these translations we see the forceful introduction to **I also consider everything to be a loss**. Here, Paul goes far beyond his former enumeration of his accomplishments and gifts. He clearly stated them to be of no value in salvation. Here he goes to the extreme of saying that **everything** is a **loss** in that matter.

Suppose you are moving to a remote jungle in Africa. You have never been there before. You pack ten trunks. There is room for nothing more. When you arrive at customs, the officers start throwing stuff out. "You will not need this." "You can't take this in." "These will not work where you are going." When you leave customs, all your goods fit in one trunk with room left over.

We all pack something into 168 hours each week. We have filled our trunks over a lifetime and are still packing. We fill some trunks with tangibles like golfing, fishing, boating, working, shopping. Others have stereos, motor homes, and automobiles. Others contain our good deeds: visiting the sick, helping the poor, a few souls won to Christ, our witness, songs of praise we have sung.

One day, when we hit customs at the pearly gates, God will examine our baggage. Trunkloads are thrown out. Possessions reduced to ashes. A few bits of service for Christ carried in. Paul describes this scene this way: **Anyone who builds on that foundation may use a variety of materials—gold, silver, jewels, wood, hay, or straw. 13 But on the judgment day, fire will reveal what kind of work each builder has done. The fire will show if a person's work has any value. 14 If the work survives, that builder will receive a reward** (1 Cor. 3:12-15).

In view of the surpassing value of knowing Christ Jesus my Lord. In this statement, Paul expresses the greatest value in his life is **knowing Jesus Christ my Lord**. The Greek word for **knowing** is a difficult word to translate. It relates to more than head knowledge. It includes the mystical knowledge of experience. It was used in pagan religions to speak of communing with the deity. Paul is speaking of the knowledge of Christ as personal and intimate. This is not to suggest that head knowledge has no place in the knowledge of Christ but that we must also experience him in a one to one faith relationship. Knowing Jesus Christ is personal and intimate.

Because of Him I have suffered the loss of all things and consider them filth. Paul is here declaring that he has already lost all things formerly of value to him. He made the decision to do away with his old life. When Paul became a Christian, he gave up a brilliant career. As a student of Gamaliel he was on the fast track to being one of the elite leaders in the Jewish religion. When he met Christ on the road to Damascus, he gladly gave up all of those ambitions. It is likely, he gave up many friends and perhaps even his family in the process.

And as he views his new life in Christ, he sees all that old life as **filth**. The Greek word here rendered **filth** can mean "excrement" (KJV **dung**). It also has in it the idea of "that which is thrown to the dogs," and is sometimes translated "rubbish," "refuse," or "garbage." This word is found nowhere else in the New Testament.

So that I may gain Christ. Here Paul declares the clear reason for his sacrifices. Gaining Christ made all the **loss** worthwhile. **Gain** is the other side of the profit and loss example.

Verse 9. **And be found in Him**. Some suggest Paul is alluding to the hour of his death, others to the time of judgment. But, it is more likely that he is thinking about his entire Christian life. Paul's use of **in Him** refers to the closest possible union between Christ and the believer.

Not having a righteousness of my own from the law. Here Paul begins discussing the difference between the idea of being saved by keeping the Jewish law and by accepting salvation as a free gift from Christ. This is the difference between being saved by works and being saved by grace. Paul says **the law** cannot provide enough **righteousness** to effect salvation. According to the Pharisees, a person received **righteousness** by keeping all the minute requirements of **the law**. It was through these outward acts that one involved himself in communion with God. Paul's Christian experience convinced him that faith alone can gain an eternal relationship with God.

But one that is through faith in Christ. Here Paul is claiming that to have a personal relationship with Christ is nothing other than having **righteousness** that comes from God **through faith in Christ**. The **faith** of which he speaks is not just a matter of intellectual understanding, but it is a matter of personal trust. He is here speaking of total dependence on God to provide salvation as a gift.

The righteousness from God based on faith is another way of stating what he had already claimed. Paul wanted to make his meaning clear. We generally call this the doctrine of Justification by Faith.

Verse 10. **[My goal] is to know Him and the power of His resurrection**. Verses 10 and 11 further explain the idea of how one can **gain Christ**. Here, again, we find that to know Him is a matter of experience and not just head knowledge. The Greek verb tense indicates that **to know Him** is a decisive act, not a process over time. A second thing Paul wants to know is **the power of His resurrection**. This is also translated **the power outflowing from His resurrection** (AMP). This describes the power of the resurrected Christ at work in the daily life of the believer. We are also reminded of the physical **resurrection** of Christ. There is no truth more powerful, when we believe it, than the **resurrection** of Christ. Knowing He arose from the grave is a life transforming experience. The **resurrection** of Christ is the primary confirmation of the truth of Christianity. This belief, produces in us the hope that we too will be raised from death. This truth, gives us strength to bear up under difficult circumstances.

Being conformed to His death. The verb translated **conformed** is found nowhere else in the New Testament, therefore a bit difficult to understand. It appears Paul was saying he would like his life and death to be formed or patterned after the life and death of Christ, including His meekness and submissiveness, as well as His unselfish love and devotion. There can be no doubt that Paul means to say that he regarded it so desirable to be just like Christ that he would consider it an honor to die in the same manner.

In the 21st century, we find Christians in many social cultures whose faith in Christ may literally bring about their death. They consider their martyrdom an honor when they consider the fact that Christ died a painful death for them. How different for most of us 21st century Americans. When we think of dying, we wish to have our death made as easy as possible.

The fellowship of His sufferings. This phrase goes hand in hand with the preceding goal. It is clear that experiencing the **resurrection** of Christ and experiencing **His sufferings** are not two separate experiences. They are two sides of the same coin. This suffering may be an inward experience or outward persecution. These two experiences suggest Paul wants to be as much like Christ as he can be. Paul is expressing the idea that he would be willing to participate in the same kind of suffering that Christ did. He wishes to identify with Christ in every possible way. He felt it was an honor to live the way Christ lived, be willing to die the way Christ died, and to suffer as need be. In today's world many are willing to wear the crown of glory but reluctant to wear the crown of thorns.

Verse 11. **Assuming that I will somehow reach the resurrection from among the dead**. A few translations use the word "if." We find that in the KJV which reads, **If by any means**. All commentators agree that this is not an expression of doubt, but of humility. It seems he is also expressing a sense of hope. This word for **resurrection** is an unusual compound word found only here in the New Testament. The word could refer to the general **resurrection** or the **resurrection** of all believers. It appears that Paul is referring to the **resurrection** when Christ returns. At that time, all believers will enter the promised state of heaven.

In summary, the Christian is to trust completely in the death and resurrection of Christ for his salvation, then spend the rest of his life imitating Christ.

Here is a paraphrase of Phil 3:7-11. **Whatever good works I thought were going to get me into heaven, I now know to be a complete waste. In fact, when I consider the absolute greatness of knowing Christ as my Lord, I count everything I ever had or did as rubbish; I have thrown it all in the dumpster. By trusting Christ (not the law) to save me, I am made right with Him. I really want to know Christ and have the power of His resurrection flow through me. I am willing to suffer as He suffered and die as He died in the hope that I will be raised to eternal life** (DLR).

CHAPTER 19

∀ Lifestyle of Victory

Many people find a special joy in watching the Olympics. In the sports world we often hear the overwhelming theme of the contestants doing their personal best. Even those who do not get a metal are pleased if they get a higher score or a faster time than their prior records. This goal is a valid concept for the Christian life. We always try to do better. We never reach perfection, but that is our ultimate goal. Let's consider what the apostle Paul says about this.

Phil 3:12-14 NIV **Not that I have already obtained all this, or have already been made perfect, but I press on to take hold of that for which Christ Jesus took hold of me. 13 Brothers, I do not consider myself yet to have taken hold of it. But one thing I do: Forgetting what is behind and straining toward what is ahead, 14 I press on toward the goal to win the prize for which God has called me heavenward in Christ Jesus.**

In verses 11 to 17, there are several allusions to the Olympic games. The Philippians were well acquainted with these concepts. Paul begins this section by saying **I have not yet reached my goal** (CEV). The Greek word for **obtained all this** is literally "received" but, it has no object. This leaves commentators divided as to what its object is. Some say it is all that is included in verses 8-11, that is, to **know Him and the power of His resurrection** (HCSB). So, Paul is referring to attaining his resurrection from the dead, or attaining the perfection he refers to right after this.

Paul says he is **not perfect**. The word for **perfect** here does not refer to any kind of moral perfection. Rather, it is best translated as "mature," "full-grown," or "complete." Paul is here wanting to make it clear that he has not become all that he wants to be. He has not accomplished all he wants to

77

accomplish. The verb here translated **have already been made perfect** appears nowhere else in Paul's writings. It is found frequently in the *Letter to the Hebrews*. The word is found often in mystery religions suggesting their sacramental rituals will bring about this highest attainment in religion. It has been said, "A mature person is a maturing person."

But I press on to take hold of that for which Christ Jesus took hold of me. I press on is another reference to the race. Paul says essentially "I keep on going." In this verse, we are reminded of Jesus Christ taking **hold** of Paul on the road to Damascus. And now, Paul is trying to take **hold** of Christ in his daily living. He is not suggesting that he does not know Christ, but that the relationship is not yet complete. The idea in **take hold** (**apprehend** KJV) is that of "seizing suddenly and eagerly." This is no doubt an allusion to the Grecian foot race as the leader reached the finish line and could claim the victory and the crown. The first word for **take hold** is active, but the second is passive. It is like he has won the race, but has not yet been awarded the crown. The crown, the prize, is yet to come.

Brothers, I do not consider myself yet to have taken hold of it. Paul is here repeating what he has just said. He uses the concept of **taken hold of** all that makes a mature Christian. The verb for **consider myself** is sometimes translated "to think." It comes from the world of commerce. It literally means "to calculate," and pictures a merchant taking an inventory or figuring the amount of a sale.

But one thing I do. Paul here gives a forceful statement expressing the singularity of his personal goal. There is no verb in this phrase. Nearly all translations supply **I do** to make it more understandable.

Forgetting what is behind and straining toward what is ahead. Paul continues his allusion to the Greek races. One running in a race would not look back to see where his competitors were. He would keep his eyes steadily forward on the goal. He did not think of the problems he faced in the past, only of what was to be accomplished in the future. The Greek word for **straining** suggests the idea of "stretching myself outward toward," that is, exerting all of one's possible effort to reach the goal.

Verse 14. **I press on** is the same verb found in verse 12. The object of Paul's pursuit is the **goal to win the prize**. The word translated **goal** is found only here in the New Testament. The **goal** continually moves forward as we press on, but yet never out of sight. It is like the headlights of a car, illuminating a segment of what is ahead, always including what we need to see. In today's world it would be the finish line of the race. The **prize** comes after reaching the goal before anyone else. In the Greek games, the **prize** was a garland, a crown, or a certificate. In today's world, it is a medal, gold, silver, or bronze.

In my youth my family often played cards: rook, bridge, pinochle, rummy, canasta, cribbage, solitaire, and perhaps a few others. These were at various times parts of our weekends and evenings. My dad and I favored cribbage.

After my children became old enough for such pastimes, they each in turn learned to play with me. After the children were grown, and particularly after I retired, Dena and I began to play cribbage together. As we played, I taught her moves to improve her game.

She beats me often. Once she said I was a good teacher. So I have the best of both worlds. If I win, I am a good player. If I lose, I am a good teacher. It doesn't matter who gets to the finish line first — I win.

In the Christian life, the prize is **heavenward in Christ Jesus** (Phil 3:14 NIV), a calling which comes *from* heaven and calls us *to* heaven. The apostle Paul often considers the possibility of his martyrdom and of his ultimate resurrection. The calling of which he speaks is that of all Christians to salvation that comes through Christ. This is our invitation to heaven. This prize belongs to all who wholeheartedly respond to God's invitation to a transforming faith in Jesus Christ.

We Christians tend to compare ourselves with others. Doing this study in Philippians may cause us to compare ourselves with the apostle Paul, or Timothy, or Epaphroditus. In comparing ourselves with them we may feel we fall short. Fortunately, I don't have to compare myself to such spiritual giants. Indeed, I have a more rigid comparison to exact. I must make a comparison between what I am and what God expects me to be. Like everyone else, I fall far short in this comparison. Paul said it best, **For all have sinned, and come short of the**

glory of God (Rom. 3:23 KJV). The good news is, God makes up the difference through His unimaginable grace. **But God has shown us how much he loves us — it was while we were still sinners that Christ died for us!** (Rom. 5:8 TEV).

Who could imagine the Eternal God dying on a cruel cross for those who failed to meet His expectations? It would not be surprising if He had died for those who met His high demands. But to die for failures — that is grace.

Here is a paraphrase of Phil 3:12-14. **Christ took hold of me on the road to Damascus. Now I want to take hold of Him. That is, I want to become completely mature in my faith. I certainly don't claim perfection at this point. I'm not looking back at what I have attained. I keep reaching out for that which I still need to accomplish. There is a prize for me at the end of this race. That prize is very simply and clearly my everlasting home in heaven** (DLR).

CHAPTER 20

A Lifestyle of Striving

The Olympic Games are good examples of the quest for new accomplishments. Figure skaters discipline themselves for hours, indeed years, to attain a slightly higher score in their competition. Those in a race, equally discipline themselves to gain but a few hundredths of a second off their former time. In a competition, like hockey, all train to beat the other team.

Everyone should have some goal in life. Those who have no goal are often looked upon as drifters. Some of us, and I include myself, have had periods of time in our lives where we had no sense of direction. We were just drifting. Most of us realize, it is only when we have some goal we want to reach or some value we want to attain, that our lives become productive.

The apostle Paul in these two verses of Scripture suggests the way a Christian should think in order to attain the gold medal in our earthly race.

Phil 3:15-16 NCV **All of us who are spiritually mature should think this way, too. And if there are things you do not agree with, God will make them clear to you. 16 But we should continue following the truth we already have.**

The Christian's primary quest to should be a daily walk with Christ. Paul gives these suggestions for obtaining that goal.

1. **All of us who are spiritually mature should think this way, too**. Think what way? For the answer to this we must go back to the previous verses. In them we find the apostle striving to become all that Christ wants him to be, acknowledging that he fall far short of perfection, but always striving.

Paul says he has not attained perfection, but it is his goal to keep running to that end, to keep pursuing perfection. We should think that way also.

All of us. Paul is here addressing others who were on the same spiritual quest. He does not consider himself to be alone in pursuit of being **spiritually mature**. This is the same spiritual maturity referred to in 3:12. He is not speaking of spiritual perfection, or sinless perfection, but of those who have attained a degree of spiritual growth but still need to grow further. Paul is certainly not suggesting that some might be completely perfect. He just admitted that he himself was not. He is suggesting that all should make the same effort that he is making to move beyond the Jewish law or any system of good works for their salvation. He is speaking to those who, like him, have experienced God's rightful claim on their lives through grace.

Should think this way, too. The word for **think** involves feeling. It includes the total thought process and experience of a human being. He is speaking of those who have totally discarded any dependence on the Jewish law for their salvation.

2. We should rely on the leadership of the Holy Spirit. Paul is saying some people might disagree with him. But if they rely on God for understanding, they will receive the truth.

If there are things you do not agree with. The Greek text suggests that it is possible that some may not **think this way**. They may not **agree** with the apostle. However, they should. Most commentators say Paul is not being arrogant. He is simply stating he knows the true way to Christ and wants all to follow it. He recognizes that some may not have been exposed to the true nature of Christianity, or some may be entertaining views that hinder their progress, or may still be hung up in the idea of keeping the law for their salvation. Some may still need to enter into the full spirit and plan of the Gospel. Some may still harbor doubts concerning the Jewish ordinances and their relationship to the gospel.

I hope the apostle is not being as arrogant as some preachers today. I have heard more often than I want to hear statements like, "You don't have to agree with me. It's your privilege to be wrong."

God will make them clear to you. Let us note, Paul is tolerant of those who do not see things the way he does. He does not see this as some grounds for battle. Rather, he sees this as an area of potential growth. He is not determined to convince them of the errors of their ways. He will leave that to Christ as they **mature** in their faith. Paul assumed that those who were sincere Christians would continue to pursue the **truth**. He is convinced that God will **make** [these things] **clear** to them and they will ultimately have a full understanding of the nature of Christianity.

How are we to know the **truth** when there are so many conflicting teachings in our world? The answer is we probably will never *know* while our feet are on this earth. But, we are to continue searching for the **truth** and following the **truth** we have. We are to search for answers in the Bible. Truth is truth wherever we find it. There is truth in archeology, astronomy psychology, biology, and lots of other "ologies." We are to incorporate all truth into our theology.

In earlier days, we heard more about the Priesthood of the Believer. This doctrine teaches that there is no go-between between man and God; no earthly priest is needed. But that doctrine also states that it is every Christian's right and responsibility to study the Bible and interpret it as he feels God leads him to do. That is our quest for truth.

3. We should continue in the truth. Verse 16. **But we should continue following the truth we already have**. Paul appears to be making a concluding remark. He has made a lengthy plea for Christians to grow toward spiritual maturity. **Following the truth** uses an imperative often translated "to walk." This is a military term and it is used "to walk in a line," or "single file." Paul is saying that having come this far we should continue in the process. We are not to lose the part of the race we have already won, but press on toward the goal.

We must recognize that different Christians have come a different distance, and on a different road, in their spiritual journey. Some are just beginning the journey and may have some immature ideas. Others may have been on the journey for a lifetime, but they are still short of perfection. The Christian journey should lead us ever forward in the everyday pursuit of living the way Christ wants us to. Anyone who is pursuing that goal is living the Christian life, even though it is imperfect. The more mature Christians should patiently teach those who are coming along after them.

In every group of Christians we will find various levels of Christian maturity. Paul tells us we should be tolerant of those less advanced in the Christian life than we are. We trust that as the less mature continue to study the Bible, and the pursuit of truth, they will find it. We should also be mindful that even the most mature among us still have room to grow. Our challenge is to continue a lifelong pursuit of truth. Let us pledge ourselves to do that.

An old English litany expresses this prayer:

> From the laziness that is content with half-truth, and
>
> From the cowardice that shrinks from new truth, and
>
> From the arrogance that thinks it knows all truth,
>
> O, God of Truth, deliver us.

Here is a paraphrase of Phil 3:15-16. **All of us who are spiritually mature should be seeking a perfection we will never attain. Now if some of you disagree with that, God will open your eyes to the truth. Now let us go on in the truth we have and continue growing** (DLR).

CHAPTER 21

A Lifestyle of Witnessing

As I grew up, our family did not attend church. The only time I was in a church building was for a few weddings and funerals. During my first year at college, I met Don. His lifestyle differed from that of most of the students. He did not drink or use profanity. Women, in his eyes, deserved respect. At that stage of my life, I was evaluating what kind of life I wanted to live. I decided I did not want to be one who gave himself to drinking, gambling, and worldly living, as many other students did.

I invited Don home with me one weekend. When he unpacked his suitcase, a large Bible sat right on top. He never spoke to me about Christ. He never asked me to go to church. His example said it all. I knew the difference between him and me was in that book.

On my next visit home, I took a little *New Testament* out of a drawer where it lay dormant since I was six. Back at school, I began reading *The Gospel According to Matthew*, I knew that Christ died for me and He had a rightful claim on my life. As the Bible spoke to me, I gave my heart to Jesus. There is great power in the written Word of God and the testimony of a Christian lifestyle.

Phil 3:17-19 NASU **Brethren, join in following my example, and observe those who walk according to the pattern you have in us. 18 For many walk, of whom I often told you, and now tell you even weeping, that they are enemies of the cross of Christ, 19 whose end is destruction, whose god is their appetite, and whose glory is in their shame, who set their minds on earthly things.**

Brethren rightly may be translated **Brothers and sisters** (NCV see discussion at verse 1:12). **Join in following my example.** Paul is here saying that his readers are to live the way he lives with a constant pursuit to imitate Christ. He is not saying this in arrogance. He knows his reputation is respected and this will be understood in the right way. Every Christian ought so to live that he can point to himself as an example of sincere Christianity, and do so in genuine humility. Few of us would live up to the example of Paul. **Following my example** is literally "become fellow-imitators of me." This is found only here in the New Testament. How many Christians today could honestly say that, "if you follow me and imitate me you'll be imitating Christ?"

And observe those who walk. The verb translated **observe** is the same as the ones used in 2:4 where we are told to **look out for one another's interests**. Basically it means "to look attentively." It means to fix one's attention on something with intensity. It comes from the word *skopeo* (skop-eh'-o) from which we get our English word "scope." In the moral and spiritual sense we should look at those who **walk** as the apostle Paul walked and imitate them.

Christians in prison are very critical of each other. They often monitor each other's behavior. They know the importance of living the testimony they profess. I often heard prisoners say, "Don't talk the talk if you can't walk the walk." Prisoners clearly know the value of lifestyle witnessing. Paul uses the word "walk" twice in this Scripture passage. Once for those who are walking the Christian life and once for those who are neglecting their Christian faith, walking like enemies of Christ. He is writing about two extreme opposites.

According to the pattern you have in us. Observe those you see walking the way you've seen **us walk**. Or, the way you've seen us live.

Here we see a shift in the object of our imitation. First we are told to imitate Paul. Now we are told to imitate others whom he includes in the word **us**. It is likely, he is here including Epaphroditus and Timothy as those who are worthy examples for imitation. **The pattern** translates a word originally meaning a mark that was made by a blow. Today, we sometimes stamp metal to give it a permanent identification. It is as though Christ made an indelible mark, like a permanent scar that could be seen by everyone.

Verse 18. **For many walk**. Here we have that word **walk** again, only this time it is talking about those who **walk** in evil ways. **They are enemies of the cross of Christ**. The cross of Christ here clearly embodies the whole story of the gospel. **The cross of Christ** is the central event in the salvation of mankind. How sad that anyone would be an enemy of this great truth. While it is not clear who these **enemies** were, Paul is not here necessarily talking about those outside the Church. Rather it is likely he is talking about those Judaizers that are mentioned several times in this book. They held fast to the Levitical law as an means of salvation. It can also refer to some Gentile Christians, particularly Epicureans, whose moral behavior was not too high. Their philosophy was "eat drink and be merry, for tomorrow you will die." Like some Christians today, they carried that philosophy into their day by day activities and philosophy. It is certainly not safe for us to **imitate** just anyone in the church. We need to select the most faithful after whom to pattern our lives. The word **enemies** comes from root word meaning "hateful" or "hostile."

Paul reminds them that he **often told** his readers about these rebellious souls. Their goal is clearly different from the goal of the apostle Paul. Paul again repeats his warning with great intensity. He is **even weeping**. The situation is so painful to him that he sheds tears while warning the followers to avoid those false teachings. The word for **weeping** describes grief that is loud and full of moaning. There is another Greek word for grieving in silence. This word describes the intensity with which Paul felt the pain of those who were **enemies of the cross**.

Verse 19. **Whose end is destruction**. Paul now speaks of the ultimate fate of these enemies of the cross. Here he writes of the inevitable outcome of their enmity. Some translations use "hell" as the equivalent of **destruction** or eternal punishment. Here we are talking about those who have no true relationship with Christ. They are hypocrites and live in the same manner as sinners of the world. A mere claim to being a Christian will not save them. Paul now describes three characteristics of their failure.

This is not to suggest that those who have had a genuine conversion experience may become lost. It is to suggest that those living such ungodly lives never had a genuine experience of transformation.

1. Their **god is their appetite**. Literally, **their god is their belly** (KJV). The word for **belly** is literally "a cavity." This

refers to more than sensuality in food, drink, and sex. It can be used of anything that attempts to fill the emptiness within. It can also refer to gaining honor, power, or influence within the political system or the Christian community. Self-indulgence and sensual gratifications is their total pursuit.

2. **Whose glory is in their shame**. Here Paul is saying that they are proud of behaviors of which they should be ashamed. You can hear them bragging about getting by with their worldly way of life. The word here translated **glory** is *doxa* (dox'-ah). It has a wide range of applications in the New Testament. Here we find it as the equivalent to "pride" or "boasting." This is the same word we looked at in 1:11.

3. **Who set their minds on earthly things**. Their whole attention is given to earthly matters. They are completely concerned with the flesh and it's lusts. They are completely lacking in spirituality. People who claim to be citizens of heaven should have their minds on heavenly things. Rather, these reprobates are thinking of ways to please themselves and other people rather than please God. These are church members who think just like lost people or they have never been saved in the first place. We leave that judgment to God. Such judgment is not in our job description.

Here is a paraphrase of Phil. 3:17-19. **Brothers and Sisters, I have set for you a good example of the Christian life. Many others also follow Christ faithfully. You should use us as examples of how to live. I have warned you often about those who are enemies of Christ. It makes me cry that I still have to keep warning you. In the end, they will be the big losers. They are headed for eternal destruction. They live to fulfill the lusts of their bodies. Then they brag about the disgusting things they do. They are completely absorbed with the pursuit of earthly pleasures and honor, missing the ultimate goal** (DLR).

CHAPTER 22

A Lifestyle of Dual-citizenship

This world is not my home
I'm just a passing thru;
My treasures are laid up
Somewhere beyond the blue;
The angels beckon me
From Heaven's open door,
And I can't feel at home
In this world anymore. – Anon.

Phil 3:20-21 CEV But we are citizens of heaven and are eagerly waiting for our Savior to come from there. Our Lord Jesus Christ 21 has power over everything, and he will make these poor bodies of ours like his own glorious body.

But we are citizens of heaven. Paul here uses a plural pronoun. **We** includes his readers that are true believers in Christ. What he says of these true believers is that we are **citizens of heaven**. This noun for **citizens** only appears here in the New Testament. However, there is a corresponding verb in 1:27. It is sometimes translated "commonwealth" or "homeland." Paul uses this political imagery to suggest that Christians are temporary residence on this earth. We believers have an eternal city, the New Jerusalem. In this city, we have fellowship with the Father, the Son, and the Holy Spirit. We will have fellowship with all the people of all ages whom Jesus Christ has made complete through His death on the cross. We confidently believe that we will be raised from death and have eternal life. Our true citizenship is in heaven. He describes this citizenship as being in opposition to those **enemies of the cross of Christ** (3:18 NASU).

The city of Philippi was named after King Philip II of Macedon, father of Alexander the Great. It was a prosperous Roman colony, which meant that the citizens of Philippi were also citizens of the city of Rome itself, and part of the Roman empire. They prided themselves on being Romans (see Acts 16:20-21), dressed like Romans and often spoke Latin (the everyday language of the Romans). No doubt this was the background for Paul's reference to the believer's heavenly citizenship. Many of the Philippians were retired military men who had been given land in the vicinity and who in turn served as a military presence in this frontier city. That Philippi was a Roman colony may explain why there were not enough Jews there to permit the establishment of a synagogue and why Paul does not quote the Old Testament in the Philippian letter.

Paul further describes the faithful as those who are **eagerly waiting for our Savior** to return. The word for **waiting** suggests "earnest and patient expectation." The faithful believe in the final return of Jesus Christ, sometimes referred to as "the second coming." This will mark the end of all earthly activities and usher all believers into **heaven**.

The Bible teaches that after the resurrection of Christ, He ascended into **heaven**. We are now **waiting for our Savior to come from there**.

Our Lord Jesus Christ makes better sense as an introduction to verse 21than an end of verse 20. This is a good place to mention how the Bible got its divisions. When the apostle Paul wrote his books of the Bible, he did not divide them into chapters and verses; none of the writers, either Old or New Testament, did. In fact, it was not even divided in words or sentences. All the Greek letters ran together without spaces or punctuation. As more people began reading and studying the Bible and comparing notes, it was found that divisions of words and passages of scripture would be convenient to locate segments quickly.

Somewhere between 1227 and 1248 Archbishop Stephen Langton divided the Bible into chapters. It was not until about 1550 that the Greek New Testament was divided into verses. Modern scholars often believe these divisions could have been better, but the current divisions are solidly ingrained and will last a long time.

Verse 21. **Has power over everything**, is literally **according to the working of his power** (YLT). **Working** translates the word *energeia* (en-erg'-i-ah), from which we get our English word "energy." This phrase continues the last part of verse 20 and introduces verse 21. The word for **power** is *dunamai* (doo'-nam-ahee). This is the root from which comes our English word "dynamite." It pictures Christ as having the complete universe under his control. It is often used for the **power** of God to transform human lives.

Paul presents a contrast to explain the purpose of the Savior's coming. In verse 19, Paul spoke of the debased nature of humanity. He is now presenting the nature of the transformation that will take place through Jesus Christ. He **will make**, that is, He will thoroughly change **these poor bodies** and make them new in our resurrection. **These poor bodies** is literally, "the body of our humiliation." Our bodies are much less than they were in creation, before the fall. Sin has taken its toll. This is no indication that our bodies are inherently evil. Rather, that they are subject to change. They get sick, die, and decay.

When Christ **comes** again, He will **make** our bodies **like his own glorious body**. Literally, "the body of his glory." Here again we have this word *doxa* (dox'-ah). It is often used to express the radiant presence of God. Here, Paul uses it to describe the nature of humanity in the everlasting life. We have not been informed as to the true nature of the body of Christ after His resurrection, but ours will be like His. It was adapted to live in the glorious world where He now dwells. It is free of all human limitations that He experienced here on earth. At Christ's coming, according to Paul, true Christians will enter into a new state of existence, and their bodies will be similar in quality and nature to the body of the exalted Christ.

The Christian concept of salvation includes both body and soul, both being completely transformed by the power of Christ. This transformation begins on earth and continues in heaven through eternity. Perhaps, we get a glimpse of this eternal transformation in Matt 17:2: **And [Jesus] was transfigured before them: and his face did shine as the sun, and his raiment was white as the light** (KJV).

By the time Jesus came on the scene, two ideas about the resurrection were firmly entrenched in the beliefs of the Jewish religious leaders. The Sadducees rejected any belief in the resurrection. They considered this irrelevant to life and was not a part of the revelation God gave to Moses. The Sadducees tried to trap Jesus by their question about the seven brothers, each of whom married the same woman in succession. Jesus corrected their view by indicating earthly patterns of marriage are not continued in heaven (see Matt. 22:23-33).

In contrast, the Pharisees believed in the resurrection. All of their beliefs are not made clear, but they believed in a life after death that required the resurrection of the body. The apostle Paul was trained and served as a Pharisee (Phil. 3:5).

We are all transients on this earth. One day, through faith, we will all come to the place for which our soul was created. We will settle down to complete satisfaction in our new home called heaven. Our transiency will end. Our journey will be complete. All the pains, worries, sadness, and struggles will be events of the past. This gives us hope. In the very midst of our deepest night, we can know that the worst things that happen to us are temporary. It is going to get better.

God looks down on our distress and says, "I see the *big picture*. You can't see it from down there." The big picture includes *forever*. One day you will join Me in My eternal Kingdom and you will see the *big picture* too.

Here is a paraphrase of Phil. 3:20-21. **We are citizens of heaven. And with eagerness and excitement we wait for our Savior to come from there. He is the Lord Jesus Christ! He is going to take our weak, imperfect human bodies and transform them into His glorious likeness** (DLR).

CHAPTER 23

ꓮ Lifestyle of Fellowship

I have found that one of the happiest places on earth is a Christian fellowship where everyone loves each other and are in harmony with each other. One of the most miserable places on earth is a Christian church where people are feuding and fighting each other. What makes it so unhappy is that the church is the one organization that is built on love. Yet, therein one finds hate and discord. That should not be. But there have been church conflicts since the earliest days. Let's see what Paul says about this matter.

Phil 4:1-3 HCSB. **So then, in this way, my dearly loved brothers, my joy and crown, stand firm in the Lord, dear friends. 2 I urge Euodia and I urge Syntyche to agree in the Lord. 3 Yes, I also ask you, true partner, to help these women who have contended for the gospel at my side, along with Clement and the rest of my co-workers whose names are in the book of life.**

Paul follows his usual custom of closing his letters with some practical suggestions and personal greetings. **So then**, appears to be an introduction to all that follows. In any case, what follows is a series of affectionate labels for his readers.

Dearly loved brothers. Again we have *adelphos* (ad-el-fos'), **brothers** or **brothers and sisters**. *Agape* (ag-ap'-ay), "dearly loved." Both of these were discussed earlier. The Greek, and some translations, include the literal phrase **longed for**.

My joy is a separate word expressing Paul's endearment for his readers. It is a strong word expressing excitement.

The word **crown** takes us back to Paul's allusion to a race. This is not the word used for a **crown** worn by a king or queen. This is the **crown** awarded to the winner of the race in an Olympic game. It would likely be a wreath placed on the head

93

of the winner. It is a symbol of honor. In today's world, it would be a gold medal.

Stand firm in the Lord is an imperative and is the same word used in 1:27. There he says, **whether I come and see you or only hear about you in my absence, I will know that you stand firm in one spirit** (NIV).

As we look here, we can visualize a soldier in the midst of a horrible battle. His purpose is to remain faithful to his purpose no matter what is going on around him. He will stand firm even to his death. This gives a picture of steadfast loyalty in our Christian faith. This pictures the phrase **stand fast**.

Dear friends is a repetition of the word for **dearly loved**. The repetition is for emphasis. **I urge Euodia and I urge Syntyche to agree**. These were apparently two prominent women in the church. What they disagreed about is unclear.

Let's see, what would two women in church argue about? Perhaps the color of the carpet. Perhaps about who should teach a certain class, or work in the nursery on a given Sunday. Or, what should be done about a teen's inappropriate dress (maybe the teen is the grandchild of one of them). Perhaps they disagree on whether the pastor should be fired or not.

Whether it was a personal issue or something theological is not too important. What is important is that their disagreement caused problems in the church. The fact that Paul used the word **urge** pointedly at both individuals, indicates the urgency of his request.

Paul called on both of those ladies, individually, to **agree in the Lord**. This phrase is literally **be of the same mind in the Lord** (KJV). By using the verb *froneoo* "to be like-minded," Paul is saying that their relationship with the Lord should cause them to get together. It is important in the Lord's work that people get along with one another. Disagreements within the church have a way of becoming known in the community. Lost people can quickly point out our animosity as contrary to our claim of Christian love. These two sisters who are disagreeing (perhaps disagreeably), each has a responsibility to get things straightened out. Such animosity needs to be taken care of quickly, lest it poisons both the church and its influence in the community.

Central to the teachings of the Bible is that we are to honor and respect each other. The world needs a spiritual witness, even if it comes in different ways. In my prison ministry, I had warm and close relationships with Catholic Priests, Jewish Rabbis, Islamic Imams, and Protestant Minsters of all varieties. Together we helped social misfits through faith in God. Did we see everything the same way? By no means! We saw similar needs and shared hope through spiritual values.

Verse 3. **Yes, I also ask you, true partner**. **Ask** is a rather strong word sometimes translated "beseech." The Greek word for **true partner** is *suzugos* (sood'-zoo-gos). It's meaning is "yoked-together." The HCSB adds as a footnote "Or *true Syzygus*, possibly a person's name." In either case, Paul is addressing some influential person to assist **Euodia and Syntyche** in finding some common ground. Here is a conflict mediator. Here, we see it is the responsibility of church leaders to step in and mediate such conflicts. This verse points to the seriousness of such division.

These women who have contended for the gospel at my side. We should be reminded here that the first hearers of the gospel in Philippi were women. Lydia was the first convert. It could be that **Euodia and Syntyche** were among those first women at the riverside and were early converts.

That these two women were fighting was the down side. Now Paul tells of their good quality. In the past, they fought for the gospel instead of fighting each other. **Contended for the gospel** uses a compound word found only here and in 1:27. Paul is suggesting that these two women fought with him side by side in the spread of the gospel in Philippi. This word is also used in the sports arena, so it could be, "we ran the race together."

Paul does not state the extent of their services. Because of the male-dominated nature of that ancient society, Paul did not permit women to preach. However, females served as deacons in the early church (Rom. 16:1). It is likely that the ministry of female members was limited to other females. Let us note that our current emphasis on equality of the sexes allows us to interpret the Bible in the context of current social settings and apply the teachings of equality found in Galatians 3:28, **[In Christ] there is neither Jew nor Greek, there is neither bond nor free, there is neither male nor female: for**

ye are all one in Christ Jesus. (KJV). God looks down and says, "There is no difference. They are all the same to me."

Along with Clement. We know nothing of this **Clement**. Commentators generally agree that this is not the famous **Clement** of Rome. **Clement** was a very common name, and it is likely he was a leader in the church at Philippi. **The rest of my co-workers** who helped in spreading the gospel. It appears the church at Philippi had grown considerably since its inception.

Whose names are in the book of life. This is the only instance of this expression in the New Testament except in the book of *The Revelation* (21:27). In the Old Testament, the figure refers to the registry of the covenant people. It clearly refers to those who are genuine Christians and through faith in Christ gained everlasting life. This is a registry of all believers who have citizenship in heaven (see 3:20).

Here is a paraphrase of Phil 4:1-3. **Therefore, my dear brothers and sisters, remain faithful in the Lord's work. I love you and long to see you, my dear friends. You are my excitement and the victory crown I receive for my work. I beg you Euodia and I beg you Syntyche, get your act together. Work together once again. And my true friend, Syzygus, help these two women to bury their differences. In the past, they worked side by side with Clement and me – and many others – in sharing the Good News. All of these now have their names written in the Book of Life** (DLR).

CHAPTER 24

A Lifestyle of Celebration

Phil 4:4-7 NKJV Rejoice in the Lord always. Again I will say, rejoice! 5 Let your gentleness be known to all men. The Lord is at hand. Be anxious for nothing, but in everything by prayer and supplication, with thanksgiving, let your requests be made known to God; and the peace of God, which surpasses all understanding, will guard your hearts and minds through Christ Jesus.

Rejoice in the Lord always. Again I will say, rejoice! Rejoice is in the imperative. It is repeated for emphasis to help Philippians face some of their discouragements. At all times, the Christian has reason to **rejoice** or be happy. When we consider that God has forgiven us for all sins and promised everlasting life, little should deter us from praising God. Consider the fact that Paul was in prison facing the possibility of death when he wrote this, yet he rejoices!

In the Lord. The happiness of which Paul speaks is found only **in the Lord**. Genuine happiness comes from within and is spiritual. The source of real joy is always **the Lord**. The character and person of God and our relationship to Him are sufficient reasons to **rejoice** in spite of temporal setbacks and problems. We maintain this happiness and reason to **rejoice** by maintaining a close day by day relationship with the living Christ.

Verse 5. **Let your gentleness be known to all men.** Different versions of the New Testament translate **gentleness** in many different ways. A few of these are: "moderation," "gentle attitude," "gentle spirit," "unselfish," and "considerate." It pictures the person who is willing to give and take rather than always standing firmly for his own rights or beliefs. This **gentleness** in spirit should be **known to all men**. That is, our Christianity should show in a kind and generous spirit to **all men**, all with whom we come in contact. The Christian should be considerate even to those who disagree with him or oppose him in some way.

This is no small challenge and the motivation for achieving it is **The Lord is at hand** (literally, "the Lord is near"). The concept of "nearness" has two possible interpretations. One possibility is that the Lord is near in proximity at all times. We are always in His presence, and therefore our behavior should reflect our relationship with Christ. The other possibility suggests the second coming of Christ is imminent. Therefore, in anticipation of that great event, we should display a Christian attitude at all times.

Verse 6 is a long and complicated clause. The YLT reads **for nothing be anxious, but in everything by prayer, and by supplication, with thanksgiving, let your requests be made known unto God**.

Be anxious for nothing (KJV). The Philippians had plenty of reasons to **worry** and be **anxious**. They lived in a society that was not particularly kind to Christians. Still, let us remember the fact that Paul was in prison giving him great reason for anxiety, if he were prone to worry. Yet in the midst of this, he advises his readers not to be **anxious**. Several translations translate the word **anxious** as **worry** (TEV). **Worry** will not change the state or condition of anything whether it is good or bad. This does not mean that we are to have no care about the issues we face in this life. We are certainly to be concerned about providing for our families, preserving good health, and in all things using good sense. Someone has said, "Worry is like a rocking chair. It will give you something to do, but won't get you anywhere."

But in everything. Paul is here talking about those things that we can pray about. This phrase does not eliminate anything. Nothing pertains to our earthly needs that should escape our prayers and trust in God. We can take anything to Him. He already knows about it anyway.

By prayer and supplication. The word for **supplication** is a stronger word than the one for **prayer**. **Supplication** infers we have some special need or want for which we need some resolution. **Prayer** suggests a worshipful attitude.

With thanksgiving reminds us that we always have something for which to be thankful. We should express **thanksgiving** when we approach God in **prayer**. The word for

thanksgiving is *eucharistia* (yoo-khar-is-tee'-ah). We looked at that word in 1:3. A thankful heart is a necessary element in sincere **prayer**. We can express thanks for favors already received, or protection in times of danger, or for deliverance from this evil world, and for another day in which to live, and also for prayers already answered.

Let your requests be made known to God. Requests are simply those things for which you ask. **God**, of course, is the object of our **prayers**. He alone can answer them. He alone deserves our faith and trust that would lead us to pray to Him.

Verse 7. **And the peace of God**. This phrase is found nowhere else in the New Testament. **Peace**, in the Bible, refers to the total well-being that comes with promise of everlasting life. It is possible only through Jesus Christ and the salvation He provides. This **peace** is found in those who have a right relationship with the living God. This **peace** should also cause healthy, happy relationships with all people.

Which surpasses all understanding. In the Greek this is literally, "which rises above all mind." We can interpret this in either of two ways. It can mean that God's **peace** will be more effective than any amount of human cleverness or careful planning. Or, it can mean that the **peace of God** is far beyond any human understanding. The Greek permits either interpretation.

Will guard your hearts and minds through Christ Jesus. **Guard** is a military term. It gives us the picture of soldiers guarding the city from invaders. Paul is saying that God's **peace** will stand like a garrison of soldiers protecting us from worries and anxieties. The **peace of God** is presented as an antidote for anxiety. The power of this protection comes from **Jesus Christ**. Apart from **Jesus Christ**, there is no protection from the evils of the world. People are helpless without Him.

In the Bible, the meaning of **heart** includes the centers of feeling, thinking, and exercising the will. The **mind** is that with which we think. Paul brings these two together to present the total personality, the wholeness, of the Christian's inner being.

Where is the hope in the midst of despair? Where is the salvation in sinfulness? Where is the upward reach when we are being pulled down? Where is the solid foundation when our world is crumbling? It is here. Dig down deep to the depths of your soul and there you will find a jewel. There it is.

Grasp it. Pull it out to the light. Hold it high and gaze on it. Smile with Joy as you behold its beauty. What is it? Jesus said it is the Kingdom of God, — that glowing, brilliant, beautiful "pearl of great price." It is a treasure more valuable than any other.

Jesus said, **The kingdom of God is within you** (Luke 17:21 KJV). Wow! Listen, my friends, here is the antibiotic to overcome the disease of sin. Here is the glow of light to overcome the despair of darkness. Here is forgiveness to wipe away all the stain of guilt. Here is everlasting life to anesthetize the sting of death. Here is the guidance system to set your life on an eternal course.

Dear Christian friend, we have that in us! Through faith in Christ and willingness to dig deep into our inner resources of faith and commitment, we will find all that God has in a store for us in this world of struggles and obstacles. Jesus said to his disciples, **Fear not, little flock; our Heavenly Father really wants to give you the kingdom** (Luke 12:32 DLR).

There is no end to the reasons we Christians have to celebrate. His concern for our daily living, His daily provisions, His constant nearness. God gives us a peace that the lost people of the world cannot understand. Our relationship with Christ is our most valuable possession.

Here is a paraphrase of Phil. 4:3-7. **Celebrate your relationship with the Lord. I say it again, celebrate! Let everyone see your gentleness and kindness. Remember that the Lord is coming soon. The Lord is always nearby. Don't get worked up about things that seem wrong. Instead, pray about everything that concerns you. And thank God for his goodness and answered prayers. Then you will experience God's peace and comfort, which exceeds anything we can completely understand. The peace of God will mount guard over your hearts and minds in Christ Jesus. God's peace will remove your anxiety and put you at ease as you trust in the Lord. Discover the peace and calm that come when Christ displaces worry in your daily life** (DLR).

ᴀ ʟifᴇꜱtyʟᴇ of Ɖaiʟy Cʜriꜱtian ʟivinɡ

Phil 4:8-9 KJV **Finally, brethren, whatsoever things are true, whatsoever things are honest, whatsoever things are just, whatsoever things are pure, whatsoever things are lovely, whatsoever things are of good report; if there be any virtue, and if there be any praise, think on these things. Those things, which ye have both learned, and received, and heard, and seen in me, do: and the God of peace shall be with you.**

Finally, brethren. This is the second time Paul has said he was coming to a close (3:1). Again, **brethren** could be translated **brothers and sisters**. In this passage we look at qualities that are valuable for both men and women. He is saying, "This is what I want you to be like."

Whatsoever things is repeated before each of six qualities Christians should possess. His repetition here adds emphasis to each of the individual qualities expressed. These qualities are as important today as they were when Paul wrote them. The apostle calls for holiness and righteousness in every aspect of the Christian's life. His list is not exhaustive, however, it covers some very important aspects of the Christian lifestyle.

True refers to all that is consistent with eternal truth. That source of truth may be from God's Word by revelation or any other source of factual knowledge. Truth is truth, whatever its source, and should be considered as a part of God's design for our world.

Honest translates a word that is much more broad than merely telling the truth. It includes being honorable and worthy of great respect. "Honored" and "worthy of reverence" begin to capture the depth of meaning in the Greek word. The Christian's life should be completely upright and worthy of

101

great respect. This does not suggest that any human should receive the reverence that belongs to God.

Just translates a word that involves innocence and holiness. It embraces the idea that we are to live in justice and righteousness before God and also our neighbors. We are to be **just** and upright in all of our dealings with all people.

Pure refers to purity in mind and also the acts of the body. It refers to whatever is chaste. It includes such unpopular words as clean, innocent, modest, and wholesome.

Lovely translates the Greek word *prosphiles* (pros-fee-lace'). Remember our *phileo* (fil-eh'-o) meaning "the love of a good friend?" Here we have *pros* "face-to-face with" and *phileo*. "Face to face with the love of a good friend." The combination reflects something that is pleasing and winsome. It relates to more than good looks. It includes attractive behavior as well, and speaks of both conduct and conversation. It pictures one who is open and transparent. Blessed is the person who has dear friends with whom he can be open and honest.

Good report translates a Greek word that is found only here in the New Testament. It means literally "sounding well." It pictures a winning personality and graciousness. A Christian's overall reputation should be of the highest quality.

Virtue suggests the qualities of mental excellence and moral integrity. The word is rarely used in the New Testament.

Praise is used describing the admiration of an individual for having done a commendable thing. Therefore, it is used in praising an individual rather than praising God.

Think on these things suggests habitual thought. To whatever extent we are responsible for our thoughts, we should keep them high and centered on God. We should hold Christian values in high regard, recommending them to others while practicing them regularly ourselves.

Verse 9 is a bit confusing. The confusion is less concerned with the meaning of the verse as with how to translate it. The word order in the Greek is **The things that also ye did learn, and receive, and hear, and saw in me, those do** (YLT). The main verb is **do** or **put into practice**. For this reason, several translations restructure the verse to put the main verb first. The TEV does this in this way: **Put into practice what you learned and received from me, both from my words and**

102

from my actions. The verb **put into practice** or **do** is in the present tense. This declares a continuous action. That is, we must keep putting into practice the things Paul taught and did. Being an imperative shows its importance.

What you learned refers to Paul's teachings and writings. Again, we remember that there was no New Testament to hold in one's hand. Various Christians had written on assorted subjects at different times. Often the disciples copied and shared these with many others. Paul is here referring especially to his own writings and teachings.

And received in whatever form they received them. They may have possessed some letters Paul had written to the other churches.

Before the New Testament canon (the choice of books included) was established, various writings circulated among the Christians. As time passed, certain of these began to have greater acceptance than others. Ultimately, around 400 A.D. the early church settled on the current 27 books of the New Testament.

And heard. It is certain that several of his readers will have heard his teachings on his earlier visits to Philippi. They recall some of his sermons.

And seen in me reminds us that Paul's life was an example through the way he lived. He lived what he believed. A part of the preacher's task is to interpret the nature of the Christian life. Another part of his task is to live it as an example. The apostle is confident that his life is a worthwhile example for others to follow.

As Christians, we want to do good things and be good examples for others. No matter how hard we try, we will fail. We will not please everyone. At times, we will not even please ourselves. Sometimes when people criticize us, we will be tempted to criticize them for criticizing us. If we do criticize them for criticizing us, they will probably follow our example and criticize even more. This is the nature of humanity — the humanity we must live with and rise above.

There is a difference between the *people of God* and *people of the world*. The Apostle Paul said, **And this is the secret: Christ lives in you. This gives you assurance of sharing his glory** (Col 1:27 NLT). What hope is there for our world except

103

the new life in Christ? A new daily experience where we respond with commitment and dedication. It is God's grace that allows us to rise above our imperfections. People become different — not because people join a church, or teach a Sunday School class, or are baptized. They become different by accepting the message of Christ as the supreme guideline for their lives. Empowered by the Holy Spirit they try to live like Christ. Then the world looks on and says, "There is a changed person."

And the God of peace shall be with you. Here we have the reward for Christian living. Paul says the way to have the blessing of God and His **peace** is to lead a holy life and to live for Christ daily. This includes serving our fellow man.

Here is a paraphrase of Phil. 4:8-9. **And now, brothers and sisters, as I close this letter, I have a few more things to say. Guard your thoughts. Fill your minds with praise and thanksgiving. Concentrate on things that are true, noble, right, pure, lovely, and honorable. Remember the things you have learned from me and put them into practice. I have taught you by my words as well as my actions. Follow these things and God, who gives peace, will be with you** (DLR).

CHAPTER 26

A Lifestyle of Contentment

Phil 4:10-14 NLT **How I praise the Lord that you are concerned about me again. I know you have always been concerned for me, but you didn't have the chance to help me. 11 Not that I was ever in need, for I have learned how to be content with whatever I have. 12 I know how to live on almost nothing or with everything. I have learned the secret of living in every situation, whether it is with a full stomach or empty, with plenty or little. 13 For I can do everything through Christ, who gives me strength. 14 Even so, you have done well to share with me in my present difficulty.**

How I praise the Lord that you are concerned about me again. There was a period when the Philippian church had no way to be of help to Paul. No one was traveling his direction. However, they apparently decided it was time to do something for him and they sent Epaphroditus with a gift. This was likely money with which he could purchase supplies. So, one of the purposes of Paul's letter is to express his appreciation for their generous gift. He never doubted their concern for him.

I praise the Lord expresses Paul's depth of appreciation both for the gift and for seeing Epaphroditus. Paul knows all blessings come from God. The gift came from the Philippians but God was behind it.

Concerned about me again comes from a single verb *anathallo* (an-ath-al'-lo). Its meaning is to "flourish again." This is a rare word. It appears only here in the New Testament. It pictures a flower putting out new roots, leaves and blossoms in the springtime. Their concern for Paul blossomed again.

Didn't have the chance to help me translates a single verb. Obstacles apparently were preventing the Philippians from sending their gifts sooner. Paul acknowledges that they wanted to help him but were unable to do so.

Verse 11. **Not that I was ever in need** shows Paul's sense of independence and contentment. He says that even while he was in prison, all of his needs were met. We often need to draw a distinction between our needs and our wants. He does appreciate the gift of his friends, but he would have gotten along without it.

I have learned how to be content with whatever I have. The phrase here is literally "In what things (circumstances) I am." By the time Paul wrote this letter, he had been through many trials and difficulties. (He enumerates several of these in 2 Cor 11:23-27.) These had taught him one lesson, that he could be **content** within himself whatever the outward circumstances. God's grace is sufficient to bear him up in all of his trials. We do not see a grumbling, mumbling, complaining Paul in the midst of his difficulties. He always finds God's love to embrace him. What more can anyone want? The adjective **content** is literally "self-sufficient." This is the only place in the New Testament where it is found. However, it is found often in Stoic philosophy and ethics. In stoicism it described the state of mind in which a person was totally independent of all other things and people.

Verse 12 is a most impressive verse. It expands on what Paul said in the last half of verse 11. **I know** refers to Paul's personal experience and it is likely repeated for emphasis. He has been through many highs and lows in his experience and they have taught him much.

I know how to live on almost nothing or with everything. **Almost nothing** is an adjective which is literally "to be abased." **Or with everything** is literally "to overflow." The idea is "to have way more than I need." Paul says he has endured both extremes and remains content in either.

I have learned the secret of living. **The secret** translates *musterion* (moos-tay'-ree-on) which comes from a Greek root meaning "to shut the mouth." This reflects the need for silence when initiated into a secret organization. The English cognate "mystery" is in this Greek word. If it is a secret, you don't talk about it and it remains mystery. The **secret of living** is a single Greek verb that means literally "I have been initiated." This is the only time it is used in the New Testament. Paul draws this metaphor from the initiation rites of the pagan mystery religions. The secret refers back to Paul's contentment with what he possessed. **In every situation** summarizes his broad areas of experience.

Whether it is with a full stomach or empty, with plenty or little. These pairs of opposites expand Paul's expression of contentment in all situations.

I often told my children their *wanter* was overactive. Of course, mine gets that way too. It appears this a basic human characteristic. Or, perhaps, it is just the American way. We always want something. Strangely, we soon tire of our coveted item. Then we want something else.

Solomon observed this three thousand years ago. He found that people who are satisfied with what they have do not suffer the turmoil of wanting something else. There will always be something you do not have. We can fret over what we lack or be grateful for what we have.

The choice is ours. We may keep wanting what we don't have. That is like trying to hold the wind in our hand. We can choose to be content with what we have. That is the satisfied life.

We can easily observe that people who are satisfied with what they have do not suffer the turmoil of wanting something else. There will always be something we do not have. We can fret over what we lack or be grateful for what we have. The choice is ours.

Verse 13. **For I can do everything through Christ, who gives me strength**. Here we have a favorite verse of many Christians. Paul here gives the source of his strength that enables him to face all situations. Paul recognizes his strength is not in himself but in his Savior. The verb **can do** is *endunamoo* (en-doo-nam-o'-o). Take off the *en* and you can see our English cognate "dynamite." Paul is here talking about his source of power. From his experience, with Christ's help, he can bear any trial, accomplish any feat, resist temptation, and accomplish any purpose Christ has for him.

Verse 14. **Even so, you have done well to share with me in my present difficulty**. Here Paul returns to his sincere appreciation for the kindness shown him through sending Epaphroditus with their gift. He did not want them to think that his independence depreciated their gift. So, he said **you have done well to share with me**, that is, you bore with me in my affliction. Their sharing with him assured him that they had not forgotten him. **But it was good that you helped me**. He notes their kindness in sharing with him in his **present difficulty**. Paul is probably thinking of both the material help they sent and also the emotional support through Epaphroditus.

Paraphrase of Phil. 4:10-14. **I really appreciate the gift you sent. I know you are always concerned about me but do not always have a way of showing it. I don't need anything right now. I have learned how to be satisfied with whatever life throws at me. I know what it is like to live with abundance and to live in poverty. I have learned the secret to being content in any and every situation. It does not matter if I am hungry or have just been to banquet, I am satisfied. With Christ on my side, I can do anything. In spite of the fact that I get along just fine whatever happens, I do appreciate your gift** (DLR).

CHAPTER 27

A Lifestyle of Giving

Phil 4:15-20 NCV **You Philippians remember when I first preached the Good News there. When I left Macedonia, you were the only church that gave me help. 16 Several times you sent me things I needed when I was in Thessalonica. 17 Really, it is not that I want to receive gifts from you, but I want you to have the good that comes from giving. 18 And now I have everything, and more. I have all I need, because Epaphroditus brought your gift to me. It is like a sweet-smelling sacrifice offered to God, who accepts that sacrifice and is pleased with it. 19 My God will use his wonderful riches in Christ Jesus to give you everything you need. 20 Glory to our God and Father forever and ever! Amen.**

In the Greek text, verses 15-17 is a single long sentence. Dividing it in more sentences gives more clarity. **Remember** calls to their attention earlier days. Many of those reading the letter would remember Paul when he was in Philippi. **You** is emphatic in the Greek. This could be translated "especially you."

When I first preached the Good News there. When Paul was on his second missionary journey, he answered what is commonly known as the "Macedonian call." This took him to Philippi. But it is most likely that he visited Philippi two more times.

When I left Macedonia. Paul is recounting some events following his initial visit to Philippi. The last place he visited in Macedonia was Berea. Opposition by the Jews forced him to leave Berea. He then went to Athens, where he had to leave in a hurry also. He needed the help of the Philippians during that time and when he was in Thessalonica. All of this was about 12 years before he wrote this letter.

You were the only church. There were other churches, but only the church at Philippi extended help. This was likely in the form of money. **That gave me help**. Paul is using commercial language talking about credit and debit. It appears that Paul is talking about more than finances. He is talking about their total relationship in which each of them gave and received from the other.

Verse 16. **Several times** translates "both once and twice." The Philippians apparently had sent monetary help to Paul on more than one occasion.

Verse 17. **Really, it is not that I want to receive gifts from you, but I want you to have the good that comes from giving**. Paul expresses appreciation. **I want ... I want** is repeated to emphasize strong contrast. Paul does not want something for himself. He wants something for the Philippians. He saw beyond his receiving a gift to their receiving a gift. The gift Paul received was money. The gift the Philippians received was the blessing **that comes from giving**. Remember Paul said, **It is more blessed to give than to receive** (Acts 20:35 KJV).

The word **gifts** translates the word "fruit," but it is also used in the sense of "interest" earned in a business transaction. Paul wants his readers to have many good works deposited in their account when they come to the final judgment.

The essential teaching of this passage is that when Christians reach outside themselves and help other people in some way, they received a blessing. Blessings are reciprocal, when we give, we receive.

Have everything is often used for the receipt in a financial transaction. A possible translation is "I have received full payment." **And more** is the same word used twice in verse 12. Here he is saying that he has more than enough. It is a verb translated "I am full." He continues to express his appreciation for the generosity of the Philippians.

A sweet-smelling sacrifice. Paul here moves from the language of commerce to the language of religion. Paul says God will see the gifts the Philippians gave him as a **sacrifice** to God. This term was originally used to describe the burnt offering which gave off an odor. God is pleased when people sacrificially give to others and He equates those gifts with a **sacrifice** dedicated to Him. Paul clearly states the **sacrifice** is to God not to him. It is good for modern Christians to realize that when they help other people they are doing something pleasing to God. **And is pleased with it** Paul is certain that God will be pleased with the sacrificial gifts of the Philippians.

My God will use his wonderful riches in Christ Jesus to give you everything you need. **My God** refers to the intimate relationship between Paul and God.

Give you. Paul does not clarify whether he means material needs or spiritual needs. It is likely he means both. The verb for **supply** (KJV) is identical to the one used in verse 18. Paul is here saying that God will fully take care of the Philippians as a reward for their taking care of him. There is always a reward for doing good. Paul is saying, God will repay them because he cannot.

Will use his wonderful riches. The riches of Christ are infinite, and they cannot be exhausted. The Philippians can have no need that God cannot meet. Paul sees it as a general principle that God is benevolent and will meet the needs of His children.

In glory. This phrase is unclear. It may refer to the manner in which God would fill their needs, such as "in a glorious manner." Or it could refer to a future state such as, "in the glorious future age." This word is again *doxa* (dox'-ah). We looked at it in verse 1:11.

Glory to our God and Father forever and ever! God and Father is literally **and to God, even our Father, [is] the glory** (YLT). It carries a sense of "to God, that is, our Father."

The word **glory**, *doxa,* in this context has the components of "praise" and "honor." **For ever and ever** describes how long people should continue praising God. Whatever praise we express here on earth will be continued through eternity while in heaven. Literally, "unto the ages of the ages."

Amen is the Hebrew word of affirmation. It means "truly" or "so be it." It is often used at the end of a prayer or to affirm something that is said.

There are a few good *lasts*. The last lesson in a series. The last hour of a workday. The last "amen" of a sermon. The last yard in a 400 meter race. The last mile in a journey home. The last chapter of a mystery novel.

Let's look at the last one. I confess. I have occasionally had to peek at the last chapter to see how the book ended. The suspense was too overwhelming. The uncertainly too disturbing. The wait too agonizing. The possibilities too troublesome. The nights too sleepless.

Have I not used words that describe much of everyday life? Overwhelming. Disturbing. Agonizing. Troublesome. Sleepless. Why do we suffer these emotions? They all speak of an unknown future.

Studying the Bible and trusting the Author, is like peeking into the last chapter. We discover everything comes out all right. That is the way life is. The plot is unpredictable. As one proceeds through the story of life, complexities often create a senseless scenario.

The Bible gives us the last chapter of life. By faith we will enter eternity with God in heaven. Knowing how the story ends, makes the difficulties in the plot more bearable.

Here is a paraphrase of Phil. 4:15-20. **You Philippians remember when I first preached the Good News there. When I left Macedonia, you were the only church that helped me out. And while I was in Thessalonica you continued to help me on several occasions. I do not say this to get you to send me more. I say it so you will get a blessing from having given to me in the past. I want these good deeds to be credited to your account.**

I have everything I need, and then some. I have abundance since Epaphroditus brought me the gift you sent. That gift was like the sweet smelling incense from the altar of sacrifice. God accepts such an offering and is pleased with it. God is going to supply all of your needs from the storehouse of His riches. In the abundance of Christ, He has everything. Now let our God and Father receive glory for ever and ever. Amen (DLR).

CHAPTER 28

Ꭿ Lifestyle of Grace

Phil 4:21-23 NASU Greet every saint in Christ Jesus. The brethren who are with me greet you. 22 All the saints greet you, especially those of Caesar's household. 23 The grace of the Lord Jesus Christ be with your spirit.

Following the conventional letter-writing custom of his time, Paul ends his letter with greetings and a benediction. However, he fills them with Christian content.

Paul begins his greetings by saying literally **Greet every saint in Christ Jesus.** The verb **greet**, a common word in the New Testament, is the word regularly used to convey greetings at the end of a letter. Its modern equivalent is, **Say hello for me to ...** (TLB), **Give our regards to ...** (MSG), **Give my greetings to ...** (NLT). Paul certainly had many friends in Philippi but he does not name them here, perhaps there are too many, he might leave someone out. He does not limit his greeting to the bishops and the elders, but includes all the members of the congregation. **Every saint**, only here in the NT does *hagios*, "saint" occur in the singular. It occurs fifty-seven times in the plural. The significance of this is that "each and every" one was to be greeted individually, person by person, name by name.

You can sense the warmth and affection shared among those early Christians. Hardship today often binds people closer together. Missionaries in countries where spreading the gospel is forbidden by governments, or other predominant religions, feel a special bond with each other.

The word **saint** is not a description of the moral character of Christians; it refers rather to the fact that they belong to God. It is therefore usually best to think of it as "God's people." In the Bible, the word **saint** refers to each one of God's believers. In this greeting, Paul is careful to include the whole Philippian Christian community with his expression of love and care.

Brethren who are with me greet you. The word **brethren** includes all his fellow Christians and is often used synonymously with God's people. This would include both men and women. It is impossible to determine who all are included in this expression, but certainly Timothy and Epaphroditus would be among them, along with all those who were fellow laborers with him. It likely included many other Christians in Rome. This may include several other Jewish believers who agreed with Paul that circumcision is not necessary for salvation.

Verse 22. **Especially those of Caesar's household**. This is significant because it shows the extent of Paul's influence. Even though he was a prisoner, he was well enough respected that the message reached people in the emperor's palace. Nero was the reigning emperor at that time. The name Caesar was given to all the emperors after the time of Julius Caesar.

Adam Clarke's Commentary says this of Nero. "Nero was at this time emperor of Rome: a more worthless, cruel, and diabolic wretch never disgraced the name or form of man; yet in *his family* there were Christians: but whether this relates to the members of the *imperial family*, or to *guards*, or *courtiers*, or to *servants*, we cannot tell. If even some of his *slaves* were converted to Christianity, it would be sufficiently marvelous. Converts to Christianity in this family there certainly were; and this shows how powerfully the Divine word had been preached and spread."[1]

Verse 23. **The grace of the Lord Jesus Christ be with your spirit**. The word **grace** in this context likely includes the free gift of salvation. It would also include the transformation that takes place when **Christ** enters the heart. The word is a catchall for all the good things given to us by our Lord Jesus Christ. The word **spirit** translates the Greek *pneuma* (pnyoo'-mah); "a current of air," "breath (blast)," or "a breeze." By analogy or figuratively it becomes "a spirit," i.e. "the rational soul."

We normally associate *grace* with God's gift to us. We do so rightly. However, there is another aspect of grace. Grace is a way of life instilled in the person who has been transformed by

114

God. We are to personify love, forgiveness, caring and acceptance. Seekers want to see an example of a Christian who is growing. Believers will respond to leadership and example better than to demands. Members look to the pastor and other mature Christians as models.

Many Christians enter Christianity through grace. They then revert to law. They serve out of duty. Some Christians demand that they and others reach a certain standard of virtue. Legalism insists we live according to *their* standards. Grace proclaims a new life because of God's forgiveness. When we personify grace, we show how God can change a sinner into a saint.

People turn from their wickedness to Christ and are changed. Bitter people become congenial. Hostile people become amicable. Hateful people become loving. The stingy become generous. The resentful become forgiving. Self-centered become outgoing. Lost to saved. Born wrong to born again. Sinner to saint. All this is accomplished by the transforming power of the living Christ. This, too, is **grace**

Several early manuscripts add an endnote regarding the timing and deliverance of the letter. These carry little weight as to their authenticity because little is known about when they were added or by whom. These subscripts give the recipients as the church at Philippi, the place of origin as Rome, and the courier as Epaphroditus (one says it was delivered by Timothy).

As often occurs, Paul ends his final statement with **Amen** (although some earlier manuscripts do not include it).

A paraphrase of Phil. 4:21-23. **Say "hello" to each and every fellow-believer you meet. The brothers and sisters I see regularly send their best wishes to you. The rest of the believers out in the community send their greetings also. All of the Christian believers in the Emperor's family add their greeting to the list. Now, may Christ's richest blessing rest on all of you. Amen** (DLR).

[1] *Adam Clarke's Commentary*, published 1810-1826 (public domain).

Study Guide

Chapter 1   A Lifestyle of Sainthood

1. How do you feel about being called a "saint?"

2. Do you feel you are "separated," "holy," and "sacred?"

3. What are the advantages and disadvantages of the Episcopal form of church government as opposed to a Democracy?

4. Do you feel your life is marked by "grace and peace?"

5. Do you find a contradiction between God being "omnipotent" and "omnibenevolent?"

Chapter 2   A Lifestyle of Continuity

1. How do you feel when you are reminded of Christian friends in your history?

2. In what areas of growth do you feel you need to work on?

3. In what way have you received special blessings by working with other Christians?

4. Have you needed to serve the Lord when you experienced personal hardship? Was that difficult?

5. Do you find it hard to forgive yourself?

Chapter 3   A Lifestyle of Right Living

1. How would you describe your love for Jesus? *Agape*? Or *Phileo*?

2. How much do you believe your choices contribute to the sin in your life?

3. How do you feel you measure up to living the "fruits of the Spirit?

4. In what ways do you, or could you, help the less fortunate?

5. Looking at the word "sincere," do you feel like that describes you?

Chapter 4   A Lifestyle of Perseverance

1. Have you Christian friends to whom you feel closer than some of your family?

2. How do you feel about translations making "brother" gender inclusive?

3. How do you feel about the questions the Chinese father asked his daughter? How do you think you would answer?

4. Is there a difference between "deep devotion" and a "martyrdom complex?"

5. Are there kinds of Christian service that would frighten you?

Chapter 5   A Lifestyle of Pure Motives

1. How do you feel when you know of others teaching things you believe to be untrue?

2. Are you often tempted to discredit another's beliefs or actions?

3. How do you feel when a famous Christian person falls?

4. How do you feel when another advances Christianity for his/her own gain?

5. Do you always consider your own motives to be pure?

Chapter 6   A Lifestyle of Ultimate Trust

1. How important is it that Christ is preached, even if the message is in error?

2. What Bible teachings do you feel are worth fighting to maintain?

3. What hardships do you endure that make you feel sorry for yourself?

4. Can you look to the future knowing God will work everything out for you?

5. How do you feel when you contemplate your own death?

Chapter 7   A Lifestyle of Trusting in Eternity

1. Under what conditions do you feel you would rather die than live?

2. Do you describe your living for Christ as a joyful experience?

3. Have you known people for whom you believed death was a welcome relief from their suffering?

4. Do you believe God has a purpose for your life, as long as you live?

5. Have you met people who believe life holds no more purpose for them?

Chapter 8   A Lifestyle of Persistence

1. How does being a citizen of heaven change your life on earth?

2. How has suffering or persecution made you a stronger Christian?

3. Do you sometimes feel you are fighting a Christian battle by yourself?

4. Do you sometimes feel like giving up?

5. In what ways are you intimidated as a Christian?

Chapter 9   A Lifestyle of Wise Choices

1. Can you accept people as they are, or do you feel the need to change them?

2. Do you consider some people beyond forgiveness?

3. Do you feel you are a source of harmony or discord in your church?

4. What is your feeling toward "fundamentalism?"

5. Do you tend to insist that your way is the right way?

Chapter 10   A Lifestyle of Service

1. How do you feel when you realize Christ gave up His heavenly home for a manger on earth?

2. Do you feel it is important that you hold on to your good name and reputation?

3. Do you feel His humiliation was an essential part of His eternal task?

4. How was it important that Christ became one of us?

5. Is being a servant important for us, as it was for Christ?

Chapter 11   A Lifestyle of Humility

1. How do you feel when you realize that Christ suffered so greatly for your salvation?

2. How do you feel when you consider the heavenly home Christ left for your sake?

3. In what ways do you feel Jesus was like us, or different from us, as He was growing up?

4. Which is harder for you to accept, the divinity of Jesus or His humanity?

5. How do you think Jesus would live if He were in 21st-century America?

Chapter 12   A Lifestyle of Devotion

1. How would you describe the feeling of "ultimate awe?"

2. How do you feel when you close your eyes and meditate on the name "Jesus?"

3. How do you feel about your lost friends when you realize that one day they will bow down before Jesus and confess Him as "Lord?"

4. What does the name "I am" mean to you?

5. How do you feel about the need to confess Christ over and over?

Chapter 13   A Lifestyle of Determination

1. Are there Christian leaders you feel you should obey?

2. Is the feeling of fear appropriate in our relationship to God?

3. How do you feel about the need to continue working for Christ for the rest of your life?

4. Do you feel God is pleased with the way you are "working out" your salvation?

5. Do you feel you are successful in living the Christian life?

Chapter 14   A Lifestyle of Joy

1. Do you enjoy, or shy away from, a Christian discussion or argument?

2. Do you feel your life is a good example to lost people around you?

3. Are you reluctant or eager to share Christ with the lost?

4. Do you feel your service for Christ is a sacrifice?

5. Do you feel that your religion is a "lift" or a "load?"

Chapter 15   A Lifestyle of Teamwork

1. Are you more able to give encouragement or receive encouragement?

2. Do you have Christian friends with whom you have a kindred spirit in serving Christ?

3. Are you sometimes more concerned about selfish matters than the cause of Christ?

4. Are you quick to judge others for what you believe is their neglect in serving the Lord?

5. When you find yourself in a crisis situation, are you sure the Lord will work things out for your highest good?

Chapter 16   A Lifestyle of Trust

1. If your parents had a reason for naming you as they did, are you living up to their expectations?

2. Do you feel your serving Christ is a kind of warfare?

3. Do you sometimes feel that troubles mount on top of each other?

4. Under what circumstances, and in what ways, do you feel Christians should be honored for their service?

5. How much risk should Christians be expected to take in their service for Christ?

Chapter 17   A Lifestyle of Christian Freedom

1. Do you tend to judge other Christians whose lifestyle does not meet your standards?

2. How do you feel when a preacher gets repetitious?

3. How do you determine whether a teacher is teaching the truth?

4. Do you believe doing good works will earn you any special status with God?

5. Do you sometimes feel like bragging about your Christian faith or service?

Chapter 18   A Lifestyle of Self-denial

1. How do you evaluate your early childhood and upbringing?

2. Have you had a life-changing conversion experience?

3. What have you accomplished that you consider of value in your Christian experience?

4. When you die, have you done any good things you want God to consider in determining your eternal destiny?

5. How do you feel about people dying for their Christian faith?

Chapter 19   A Lifestyle of Victory

1. In competition, how do you feel if you win? Or lose?

2. Do you feel you are a mature Christian?

3. Do you feel you and God have a hold of each other?

4. What would you consider the ultimate prize here on earth?

5. Do you tend to compare yourself with other people? If so, how do you come out?

Chapter 20   A Lifestyle of Striving

1. List a few goals you hope to attain during the rest of your life.

2. On a scale of 1 to 10, where would you place your spiritual maturity?

3. How sure are you that you know THE truth?

4. In what areas do you feel you still need to grow?

5. Can you patiently help others in their pursuit of truth?

Chapter 21   A Lifestyle of Witnessing

1. How do you feel, realizing when people want to imitate Christ, they should be able to imitate you?

2. Are there other Christians whom you believe are worthy of imitation?

3. Do you weep when you see other Christians living ungodly lives?

4. Do you hear Christians brag about things of which they should be ashamed?

5. How should you relate to church members who are living worldly lives?

Chapter 22   A Lifestyle of Dual-citizenship

1. How do you feel about the possibility of Christ's imminent return?

2. Do you feel God controls both the good and the bad events in our lives?

3. What do you think our bodies will be like in heaven?

4. How does your dual-citizenship affect your daily life?

5. To you, what will be the best thing about heaven?

Chapter 23   A Lifestyle of Fellowship

1. Are there Christians you have helped grow in their faith that you would consider your crown?

2. In what areas do you feel the need to stand fast in your belief or behavior?

3. Are you aware of a Christian fellowship being broken by discord? How do you feel about that?

4. In the midst of Christian conflict, are you more apt to stay out of it? Get involved in it? Or, try to heal the rift?

5. Are you now working side by side with other Christians to further the Kingdom of God?

Chapter 24   A Lifestyle of Celebration

1. How do you rejoice when you don't feel like rejoicing?

2. Do you find it easy to be gentle with those who cause you problems?

3. Do you have problems over which you feel anxious? How do you handle those feelings?

4. In your overall response to life, do you feel you have peace?

5. Do you feel free to pray about anything and everything that concern you?

Chapter 25   A Lifestyle of Daily Christian Living

1. Of the Christian behaviors listed in the lesson, which do you feel are the most difficult to live up to?

2. Do you feel it is possible to keep these constantly in your thoughts?

3. How well do you believe you would understand or practice the Christian life if you did not have a Bible to guide you?

4. Can others learn what the Christian life is like by looking at and imitating you?

5. How do you feel reflecting on these penetrating questions?

Chapter 26   A Lifestyle of Contentment

1. Are there people in our world that you would like to help but know of no way to do so?

2. Are you aware of people who have a special concern for you?

3. Can you find contentment even when things are not going well?

4. How do you feel when you see starving children in third world countries? Could you find contentment living in those circumstances?

5. Have you received special gifts which you cherish from Christian friends?

Chapter 27   A Lifestyle of Giving

1. Do you sometimes feel you are asked to give to causes that really do not need your support?

2. How do you feel about the statement, "Don't give until it hurts – give until it feels good?"

3. When you give to Christian causes, do you feel you are giving to God?

4. Do you give for the purpose of receiving?

5. Do you believe your gifts for Christian causes have eternal value?

Chapter 28   A Lifestyle of Grace

1. Would you dare to try naming all the people who have been a blessing to you?

2. Do you feel it is important that Paul did not limit his greeting and gratitude to the leaders only?

3. Have you had hard times that brought you closer to God?

4. Do you feel living with grace in your lifestyle describes you?

5. How do you feel about coming to the end of this study?

Index

Abraham, 68

abundance, 108, 112

abundant, 55

abuse, 67

account, 71, 110, 112

acquittal, 60

Adam, 114, 115

adelphos, 13, 93

affection, 5, 9, 13, 39,49, 59, 113

affirmation, 49, 111

Afghanistan, 35

Africa, 11, 73

agape, 9, 10, 93

agenda, 18, 19

agitators, 19

Alexander, 61, 89

altar, 56, 112

ambivalence, 27

America, 14, 31, 38, 61

American, 29

Americans, 52, 75

America's, 29

anathallo, 105

angels, 48, 89

anthropos, 3

Antichrist, 40

Aphrodite, 61

apologia, 19

apostle, 3, 5, 14, 16,18, 21, 22, 29, 34, 40, 49, 56-58, 62, 63, 65, 66, 77, 79, 81, 82, 86, 87, 90, 92, 101, 104

apostles, 31, 62

apostle's, 39

apostolos, 62

Aramaic, 69

Archbishop, 90

archeology, 83

Aristotle, 19

arrogance, 19, 35, 63, 86

astronomy, 83

Athens, 109

athlete, 55

athletic, 31, 56

Augustus, 44

authenticity, 68, 115

awe, 40, 52

Bangkok, 42

Baptist, 42

baptized, 1

baptizing, 14

Beijing, 29

belief, 12, 29, 32, 70, 72, 75, 91

beliefs, 19, 21, 70, 91, 92, 97

believe, 14, 16, 31, 35, 39, 46, 47, 59, 64, 70, 75, 89, 90, 113

believed, 14, 29, 39, 46, 69, 71, 92, 104

believer, 7, 55, 74, 75, 115

believers, 1, 13, 15, 18, 52, 54, 55, 70, 76, 83, 89, 90, 113-115

believer's, 90

believes, 50

believing, 27, 29, 31, 32, 39

benediction, 113

benevolent, 111

Benjamin, 65, 68, 70

Berea, 58, 109

Bishop, 1

bishops, 113

blessed, 32, 103, 110

blessing, 4, 104, 110, 112, 115

blessings, 6, 105, 110

boast, 33, 35

boasted, 35

boasting, 36, 69, 88

boldness, 23

bond-servant, 37

bond-slave, 40

brethren, 18, 65, 85, 86, 101, 113, 114

brother, 13, 61, 62

brothers, 4, 13, 14, 16, 34, 70, 77, 78, 86, 88, 91, 93, 96, 101, 104, 115

Buddhism, 71

caco, 67

129

Pastoral, 59

pastors, 55, 60

perfection, 38, 77, 78, 80-84

peritome, 67

persecute, 32

persecuted, 69, 70

persecuting, 65, 69

persecution, 14, 31, 69, 76, 113

Perseverance, 13

Peter, 10, 32

Pharisee, 65, 69, 70, 92

Pharisees, 69, 74, 92

polis, 30

polites, 30

Pope, 2

preachers, 17-19, 82

preaching, 18, 21, 57, 59

preincarnate, 37, 38, 43

pride, 28, 35, 53, 55, 69, 88, 90

priest, 18, 83, 56, 95

Prophets, 10

proselyte, 68

prosphiles, 102

Protestant, 95

psuchee, 35

Rabbis, 95

Redeemer, 43

redemption, 38

resurrection, 3, 10, 40, 43, 71, 75-77, 79, 90-92

revelation, 91, 96, 102

reverence, 44-46, 50, 52, 102

reward, 27, 32, 73, 104, 111

riches, 61, 109, 111, 112, 115

right, 9, 12, 23, 26, 27, 33, 35, 36, 51, 63, 68, 76, 77, 83, 85, 86, 99, 104, 108, 112

righteous, 12, 16, 41, 102

righteousness, 9, 11, 12, 36, 54, 65, 69-71, 74, 101, 102

ritualistic, 62, 67, 68, 72, 78

Roman, 1, 2, 5, 11, 14, 15, 31, 44, 61, 89, 90

Romans, 90

Rome, 15, 17, 18, 27, 35, 57, 61, 89, 96, 106, 114, 115

sacramental, 78

sacred, 1, 69

sacrifice, 3, 6, 53, 56, 62, 63, 109-112

sacrifices, 56, 74

sacrificial, 56, 110, 111

Sadducees, 91

Sainthood, 1

saints, 1, 15, 30, 48, 113

Satan, 31, 62

Saul, 68

savior, 14, 22, 28, 43, 47, 70, 89, 90,, 91 92, 108

Self-indulgence, 88

selfish, 17, 19, 33, 35, 36, 39, 40, 58

self-centered, 19, 36, 63

self-confidence, 6, 19

self-control, 12

self-deceit, 35

self-denial, 59, 71

self-destruction, 63

self-glory, 63

self-love, 63

self-righteousness, 36

self-seeking, 19

self-serving, 59

self-sufficient, 106

seminary, 5

sensual, 88

Septuagint, 46

Sheol, 46

shepherd, 2

Silas, 1, 58

Simon, 10

skopeo, 86

slave, 38-40

slaves, 15, 59, 114

soldier, 43, 61, 62, 64, 94

soldiers, 15, 99

soteria, 22, 49

soul, 10, 22, 26, 33, 35, 39, 57, 58, 69, 91, 92, 100, 115

souls, 35, 46, 73, 87

sovereignty, 47

spendo, 56

Stephen, 69, 90

sumpsuchos, 35

sunathleo, 31

suzugos, 95

synagogue, 1, 90

About the Author

After retiring from 25 years as a correctional chaplain in August 1986, Reverend Rowley served in a variety of ministry activities. Reverend Rowley was Visiting Lecturer in Psychology at Greenville (Illinois) College during the 1986-87 school year. For several years he taught Psychology part time for Lakeland Community College and Greenville College. Following retirement, he and his wife, Dena, went to the People's Republic of China for the summer of 1987 to teach English at Yunnan College of Education in Kunming. During the fall of 1990, he and his wife taught English in Bangkok, Thailand. In 1992, he served as a volunteer pastor in Hawaii. 1993 Dale and his wife served as volunteer counselors in Mongolia and China. They spent the month of October 1996, in Ivory Coast, Dale trained prison workers, Dena taught English.

On various occasions he has served as pastor, chaplain, college teacher, interim pastor, conference leader, supply preacher, pastoral counselor, conflict mediator, Christian writer, and other pastoral ministries.

Since his retirement. Reverend Rowley has written for a variety of Christian magazines. He has also written Sunday School curriculum materials for LifeWay Christian Resources. This is his fourth book. The other three being: *Cherry*

Blossoms: Memories of Bert I Cherry; A Manual for Pastoral Search Committees; and Ecclestiates: Down to Earth.

Reverend Rowley was born and reared in Topeka, Kansas. He graduated from Oklahoma Baptist University, Golden Gate Baptist Theological Seminary, and Southern Illinois University. He has one baccalaureate and three masters degrees. He has completed several quarters of Clinical Pastoral Education.

Dale and Dena have four children (one deceased), six grandchildren, and six great-grandchildren.